The
Silent Miracle

D1304378

The
Silent Miracle

Awakening your true spiritual nature
by stilling your mind

RON RATHBUN

BERKLEY BOOKS, NEW YORK

THE SILENT MIRACLE

This book is an original publication of The Berkley Publishing Group.

A Berkley Book / published by arrangement with the author

PRINTING HISTORY
Berkley trade paperback edition / January 1999

The Penguin Putnam Inc. World Wide Web site address is http://www.penguinputnam.com

ISBN: 0-425-16678-3

BERKLEY®
Berkley Books are published by The Berkley Publishing Group, a member of Penguin Putnam Inc., 375 Hudson Street, New York, New York 10014.
BERKLEY and the "B" design are trademarks belonging to Berkley Publishing Corporation.

PRINTED IN THE UNITED STATES OF AMERICA

10 9 8 7 6 5 4 3 2 1

Gratitude and Appreciation

To my wife, Lavana, for her love, devotion, and unwavering diligence in the editing process. Without her by my side, my pathway would have been far more difficult and far less beautiful.

To my eternal friend and mentor Gene, who introduced me to stillness of mind, the pathway of self-understanding, and the infinite beauty of the spiritual world.

To our dear friend Sheri Wachtstetter, for the beauty of her true nature watercolor paintings on the chapter title pages.

To Paul and Claudia Riha of Stone Imagery, for their attention to detail and dedication to excellence in the artwork preparation and for creative advice.

To my literary agent and friend Julie Castiglia, for her patience and editorial expertise.

To Denise Silvestro, our editor, having you appear in our lives was a blessing. Thank you for helping to polish our diamond.

To Dave Harvey for his friendship and gentle persuasion and encouraging me to continue teaching what I know to others.

To each and every one of my students; through you I have learned and continue to learn how truly powerful The QM Practice is.

Contents

Contents

Preface

Much of what people can learn from life falls on deaf ears because of daily pressures and busy lifestyles. In trying to achieve so much in the material world, many have lost touch with what is important—the ability to feel contentment in life. We are bombarded with messages about who we should be, what we should want, and how we should be getting it. Our minds become filled to capacity and we feel overloaded. Life becomes an unending race toward achievement, leaving us little or no time to relax and enjoy. This is the way to burn out: too much doing and not enough being.

You can change!

It is hard to believe you can feel better than you ever imagined, and yet a silent miracle can happen to anyone; all it takes is a few simple steps over a period of time. The first step is learning to calm your mind. It is so simple, it is often overlooked. To realize the silent miracle, all you have to do is practice for ten minutes in the morning and ten minutes in the evening in the privacy of your own home. This method is not tied to a specific religious philosophy; you can benefit from it no matter what you believe. This practice will simply help you to release resistant thoughts that keep you from experiencing love in your life.

The Silent Miracle offers a practical way to slow down your thoughts, relax your mind, and be at peace with yourself. This practice will show you how to release emotional problems in a seemingly miraculous way. As you begin to do The Quiescence (to become quiet) Meditation Practice, you start to notice subtle changes that, with time, grow in magnitude. Upon learning to liberate yourself from your most obvious psychological baggage, you will realize that you are no longer being distracted by, or wasting time on, annoying thoughts and feelings; therefore, you will have more free time to enjoy yourself. It will seem as if time appears out of nowhere because you are no longer being consumed by your problems. You will begin to have time to *really* live your life and feel your connection with yourself and the world around you. You will begin to see sunrises and sunsets as if for the first time. You will begin to notice the wind caressing your face. You will become more aware of the beauty of nature. All of life will appear sharper and more vibrant because your mind is calm enough to experience and feel the magnificence surrounding you.

My goal in writing this book has been to help people experience life by simply being more mindful in the moment. By learning to sit down for a few minutes each day to still your mind, you will find what everyone is looking for—a life to be enjoyed. Lasting happiness, and an intimate connection with all that life has to offer, is the result of uncovering your true spiritual nature.

Introduction

If you look carefully at your relationships with people, you will realize that the most beautiful and most traumatic events in your life have to do with the giving and receiving of love. Everyone's motivation, deep down inside, is a need to feel love, give love, and be loved. To love, you first must be able to listen with your mind to what your heart is telling you.

Do you listen to your heart with your mind?

A quote from my first book, *The Way Is Within*, is very appropriate here: *There are many words to be said about this or that, but when love is not one of them, oh what an emptiness it can bring you.*

Your initial experience of love is from your parents or the people who raised you, and from their philosophy of life, your perception of love is born. Your parents, with all of their good intentions, can give only what they have within themselves. They cannot give what you are really looking for: the understanding of who you are, nor can they learn the lessons of life for you.

Growing up is never an easy thing to do, and as a teenager, I had no idea who I was. After graduating from high school, I worked in a hospital. During this time I met a beautiful young girl and fell in love with her. I honestly felt I had found love, but I was painfully shy and too insecure to express my feelings. Nevertheless, we became friends and the love I felt was to the depth of my soul. One day, after being close friends for what seemed a long time, she informed me that she needed space and our relationship ended. I was heartbroken. The emotional pain and loss that I experienced was intense for months and lasted well into the next year. Without her presence I felt empty inside. I had no understanding of who I was or what life was about. The warm feeling of love inside me was gone. I asked myself, "Where did the love inside me go?" I had no answers, only questions, and a great pain in my heart.

How do you give to yourself what you are supposedly giving to another? How was I going to find the love that I did not have for myself?

I did not like how I felt. I tried finding solace in material possessions. I quickly realized that they were inanimate and did not offer the fulfillment my soul so desperately needed. So I began searching, trying to find who I was within, but I didn't know where to begin looking. I recognized that I needed a teacher who could answer my questions. I explored many different organizations and studied with a number of people. I tried a myriad of ways to release myself from my inner turmoil, but my problems remained.

One day I met a man who became my teacher, mentor, and friend. He introduced me to a form of meditation called *stillness of the mind*. I began to practice stilling my mind and my life began to calm. I studied with this man for many years and learned many valuable lessons that opened up a spiritual world. Yet ultimately I knew my answers must come from within me. The knowledge I had acquired helped me to understand the bigger picture of life, but something was missing: my true nature still eluded me.

Eventually I reached a point in my own personal growth and development, after fourteen years of study and becoming an ordained minister, where it was necessary for me to study alone. I wanted to explore more about my mind and the unresolved problems within me. I became even more diligent and aware of what my mind was doing as a result of meditation, and what I found startled me. It was complex and simple at the same time. I came to realize there was a series of reference points in my mind, points of energy. I became aware of a tangible relationship between brain function and mind function and what comes from directing one's conscious awareness to a still point. I found a way to release myself from my resistance to life—resistance that was binding me to painful, nonproductive, and sometimes self-destructive behavior patterns. I understood, through the clarity of my own mind, why I was doing the things I did and learned how to release myself from those lifelong habits that had haunted me my whole life. Everyone has had negative childhood experiences that manifest themselves in adulthood as emotional "buttons of resistance," or unhealthy, dysfunctional behavior patterns. Whenever you react to someone or a situation with fear, anger, anxiety, doubt, depression, defensiveness, or hatred, for example, your buttons are getting pressed. These negative emotions can have effects that range in intensity from a mild response to a full-blown overreaction.

Through many years of study, I developed a workable system of meditation that releases dysfunction. From doing The

Quiescence Meditation℠ (QM) Practice for merely twenty minutes a day, you will learn to cultivate your true nature. You will learn to release yourself from self-defeating mental programs and your own buttons of resistance forever. The solutions to the most complex problems in your life will become obvious when you know how to direct your conscious awareness to a still point within. Best of all, you will find who you really are and experience true happiness and love. The Quiescence Meditation℠ Practice simply allows silent miracles to happen in your everyday life. All that is needed is for you to do the daily practice, live your life, and allow your mind to open to your heart.

The
Silent Miracle

*The physical world
is a mere reflection
of each person's
individual perception of life.*

One

How Does the Outside World Influence You?

WACHTSTETTER

*Why does the material world,
bring you only
a fleeting form of happiness?*

Everywhere in the world people are looking for happiness and a sense of well-being, but most people do not know where to find it. Our society says if you have a good job, lots of money, a good relationship, a nice house, and a new car, you are successful and should be happy, but often something seems to be missing.

If being yourself does not produce happiness, you will forever chase happiness and never experience it. When man-made things are more important than finding your true spiritual nature, unhappiness and discontentment will be close by. Man-made things become distractions, and what we have becomes more important than who we really are. The more we have, the more we want, but it is never enough.

Where does it stop? It will stop when you let go of material things and use possessions for what they really are, tools in the outside world.

The true answers in life are so easy, and yet they elude most people.

When will our society recognize that being a loving person is the most important goal to attain and where true happiness is found?

Change in the world will come when everyone stops for a few minutes every day to look within and start solving their own problems, instead of inflicting their disharmony on others.

Stop thinking for a few minutes each day and break your attachment to the outside world. Feel who you are. In a single moment of silence, your whole life can change, if you just pause for a couple of moments each day.

*When you finally
do not need possessions
to make you happy,
you can learn to enjoy them
simply for what they are.*

A child walking down the street puts his hand in his pocket and pulls out a marble. What determines the value of a marble in a child's mind? Is it in the possession of the marble or is it just that it's a pretty glass ball? The fun and worth is not in the ownership, but in the simple joy it brings. That the marble is lost in a game does not matter if you had fun while playing with it.

Marbles may be lost or marbles may be won, but there are always more to be had. It is strange but true: when you do not worry about losing something, you can really enjoy it. Do not carry the weight of objects in your mind or it will cost you in how you enjoy yourself.

Does it help to carry anything that makes you unhappy? Let go of your need to possess things. Our obsession with material acquisition is a distraction. Yes, some things are necessary for survival—shelter, food, clothes to keep us warm—but the desire to obtain things in excess comes at a high price. If you do not like how you feel, it is time to go to work in a different way. It is time to work on the only thing you truly possess—yourself. It is time to find out why you are attached to things that are not a part of you. Detachment is one of the most important lessons that each individual must learn in order to be free. Without detachment we are bound to something that is not a part of who we are.

Only when the love in your heart is more important than possessions will you have a chance to be truly happy.

Who are you
without
your physical possessions?

There are many games that individuals in society have collectively become used to playing and have forgotten that they are games. The game of ownership is one of the single biggest distractions to the spiritual evolution of humanity. In the deep spiritual sense, you cannot own anything.

Tragically, the American Indians suffered at the hands of a world that played the game of ownership. They could not understand that someone could put stakes in the ground, draw up a document, and declare, "I own this." To the indigenous people, this game did not make sense. How can anyone own a part of the earth?

To the early settlers of North America the law was, whoever first occupied the land owned it. It's ironic; weren't the American Indians already living on the land? From the American Indian point of view, no one could own land.

What we run into here is the difference between man-made law and spiritual law. Which one is real and in harmony with nature?

The key to happiness is living your life according to natural laws. It is true that we still must play society's games, but we do not have to be mentally imprisoned by them. To have nice things that bring comfort in our lives is not wrong. But when you attain anything at the expense of others, or when your possessions become more important than your spiritual well-being, you will suffer. When you mentally free yourself from what you can never really possess, you will feel true freedom and a connection with nature.

End the suffering. Love people, not things!

*Greed is unfulfilled craving
in extraneous acquisitions
and inevitably a pathway of destitution.*

Greed is a form of destitution, an insatiable need that consumes our soul and infects our entire life with negative energy. Greed stems from insecurity, a feeling of incompleteness that we try to compensate for with acquisitions or approval from others.

It is sad to say, but uncontrolled desire is the motivating force behind much of our society's disharmony. We work harder so we can make more money; we want more money so we can buy more possessions. We want more possessions so we can have more power. More, more, more. Where does it ever stop? When is there ever enough?

Greed is impelled by fear: fear of losing your material possessions; fear that without your possessions you have no worth; fear that without possessions there is nothing to sustain you. When the material world slips away, all that remains is what is within you. How frightening to think that there is no sanctuary within. What is within you is of a far greater wealth than inanimate objects can ever provide.

Material wealth looks good in the outside world but means nothing if your heart is held captive by the psychological monster of greed. Excessive behaviors can only be conquered by facing your fears—fear of losing your possessions, fear that without them you are worthless. Let go of the outside world of possessions and the monster of greed will wither away. When freedom from possessions is finally won, greed will disappear, and you will be rich beyond compare.

*Possessions are like sand castles,
beautiful to behold
but easily swept away by the sea.*

The fun of a sand castle is in the building, all the while knowing that one strong wave can sweep it away. Treat material possessions as if they were sand castles—fun to create, pretty to look at, impossible to control. If you are driven by the need to possess, belongings will run your life and you will never know the joy that our world can bring. You'll always be worrying about the next wave, futilely trying to hold back the tide.

Isn't it amazing how you can spend most of your time desiring possessions in hopes of a fleeting moment of happiness that can be gone in an instant? If you are truthful with yourself, you will recognize that what you are looking for is a feeling of fulfillment. We all want fulfillment, but where we look for it is each individual's choice. If you are searching for happiness in material wealth, you will be sorely disappointed. Objects cannot fill a void within you. Possessions don't make you a contented person.

When possessions rule your life, your world is fragile, your existence is shallow, because you cannot access your heart. When an inanimate object has command over your emotions, it not only feels like hell, it is hell! Only when your attachment to possessions is eliminated can you find fulfillment.

If you are seeking love and self-acceptance in anything other than your own heart and soul, you will be destined to search endlessly—a life lived in constant pursuit of an illusion.

*When a conscious sense of value
is realized and lived
everyone in the world profits.*

Whatever your occupation in the world, be there and do the best you can. Make your life a meaningful one.

For what reason would you ever hold back and intentionally not do a good job?

How much effort does it take to do good work?

It is so much more difficult to not live up to your potential. Anytime you do less than your best, you suffer internally. If what you do is inferior, someone else will have to rectify your carelessness. When you perform the finest work you can, there is never a reason to feel guilty or worried. Having fewer worries weighing you down enables you to focus on the job at hand and work more efficiently. Efficiency gives you more time. With more time comes increased quality and productivity. It's a no-lose proposition—if you do your best, you'll do a terrific job. What really matters is that *you* know you gave it your all.

Everyone has a responsibility to themselves and to the world they are a part of. Put your heart in what you do. Putting your heart into your work is like being paid in contentment. You are rich in the way you do things and how you experience life. When your conscious sense of value is developed to the highest order and felt within, you will find yourself enjoying almost everything.

Your conscious sense of value has to do with how you see yourself—how you appreciate who you are and estimate your worth. When your conscious awareness connects with your true spiritual nature, your self-worth rises to the purest standard. In effect, you acquire an exemplary sense of value—how you see yourself—and everyone in the world profits.

*All disharmony on the planet
is a direct result of troubled individuals
who inflict their internal problems
on the world.*

All disharmony on the planet is a direct result of unenlightened thinking which leads to ignorant actions. Disharmony always originates as an individual problem but ends up as a collective one. One person will crave something so badly he will lie, steal, cheat, or compromise another's life to get his way. Any individual who loses control of his mind, cannot control his behavior, and interferes with the rights of another must be incarcerated by society.

Why does this happen? The answer is locked up in his mind.

But how does one understand the contents of one's mind?

And how do you change the condition of the mind?

It must start by calming negative energy with a serene, subtle form of energy. A kind of energy that can diffuse complex confusion. This energy is stillness within the mind. Stillness transforms disharmonious conditions. Practicing Quiescence Meditation in the privacy of your home calms your disposition, calming you and those around you, enabling you to contribute to society instead of being a burden on it. This is the key to mankind's salvation and can only happen within each person who consciously chooses to attain inner harmony.

Without a sense of value about yourself, how can you have a sense of value about anything?

When kindness for yourself is coupled with quietude each day, your life can change. The QM Practice offers a beautiful way to begin understanding who you are, for yourself, from within your own mind. It is the only way I know of.

*If mankind were not on the planet
there would be no pollution,
no overpopulation,
and no disruption of the animal kingdom.
What does this say about mankind?*

Everything man-made is a reflection of the minds that created it. We are creating all of the time, with everything we do, everything we say, and everything we touch. Every expression in your life has meaning. What you express is determined by what you think and how you feel.

What do you know about your thoughts and feelings?

Far too many minds are too busy. The average person has two, three, or four thoughts occurring at once. We are bombarded with excessive information, toxic messages, and unrealistic expectations. We are told what to do, how to do it, and that we should have done it yesterday. With all of this activity, the mind becomes a mass of frenzied energy, which in turn becomes the world's energy. Uncontrolled thought energy is the reason why there are so many problems on the planet.

You have the power to help bring about positive change in our world. You can make a conscious decision to clean your inner landscape of the debris that pollutes your mind and poisons your soul. Slow down your mind and you will undo the problems you have created for yourself and our world. Quiet your thoughts and clear your mind, to a still point within.

Look in the mirror; do you like what you see?

*When the mind is familiar
with an appreciation of beauty,
thoughts and feelings merge
as a vibrant self-expression of life.*

Two

What Do Your Thoughts Mean?

*In the mind's most basic terms,
there are only two things in the universe,
you and everything else.*

Your relationship with yourself determines how you relate to everyone and everything around you. Are you in harmony or in pain and suffering?

Awareness of your thought process is necessary if you are to understand yourself and your connection to the outside world. Thoughts are incredible; they literally make up your whole world. You cannot do anything without first thinking!

What do you know about your thoughts and where do they originate?

Why do some thoughts bring happiness, while others bring grief?

What is the relationship between your thoughts and feelings?

We are all an outgrowth of our past, and every day we make decisions based on previous information. Everything we do today in some way correlates to how we did something in the past.

But what if the information from the past is flawed?

How do you correct this faulty information?

The Quiescence Meditation (QM) Practice is a process of learning how to release yourself from the binding chains of the past that keep you in repetitive patterns.

Contemplate the thoughts that dictate your behavior.

How many distinct kinds of thought are you aware of?

And what kind of thoughts dominate your thinking?

When you begin to understand the connection between what you think and what you do, you will start to unlock many mysteries within your own mind.

*Negative emotional patterns
are mental disorders
often passed from adults to children
and unintentionally accepted
through lack of experience and awareness.*

One of the first observations you will make when you begin The QM Practice is how busy your mind is and that calming it is not easy. What you are experiencing is the resistance from your emotional patterns. Emotional patterns can be expressed by any dysfunctional behavior: fear, anger, worry, selfish craving, jealousy to name a few. These behaviors are manifested when "emotional buttons" are pressed, when certain events trigger unconscious reactions within us.

Emotional patterns are passed from one generation to another. Young children are naturally open and receptive, and buttons are inadvertently installed in a child's mind by his parents or whoever influences the child as he is developing. Children, not knowing any better, learn behavior through inference. Once a button is established, it becomes a repetitive pattern. Every time a button is pressed, the original reaction is repeated in a closed loop of negative thought followed by an action. Negative patterns are counterproductive, causing emotional pain and suffering each time a button is pressed. Oddly enough, our society often views a temper, a mood, or a bad attitude as acceptable behavior instead of the dysfunction it is.

Consciously watch your thoughts. Think about what you are observing when you react and you will recognize when a button fires. When you feel a bad mood coming on, relax and you will begin the process of diminishing the energy feeding your patterns.

*There are two basic types
of mental energy—
resistant thought
and nonresistant thought.*

All thoughts are mental energy. Although there are many kinds of thoughts and each one affects us differently, there are only two basic types of mental energy: resistant thought and non-resistant thought.

All negative thoughts such as fear, anger, worry, hate, or jealousy produce resistance in life. The negative energy created by these thoughts gives birth to an emotional button. Each time a button is pressed, it calls to mind the original negative experience and reproduces the original negative reaction.

Ponder this: If the emotion from a button lasts for, let's say, two hours and is activated one hundred times over your lifetime, one incident can consume two hundred hours of your life! And this is just one button!

All nonresistant thoughts such as love, kindness, and compassion liberate you from the predicaments in life. These thoughts always promote peace and harmony. The true nature of our being is nonresistant energy. Allow the true nature of your essence to emerge, and nonresistant thoughts will bring happiness and well-being.

As you begin The QM Practice, you will learn to release resistant thoughts and the problems they create forever.

*Internalized fearful emotions
from the past
often become chronic headaches
in the present.*

The following is a case history of one of my students. This particular woman suffered from a combination of chronic migraines and intestinal discomfort. I recommended she see me so I could investigate the energy pattern associated with her headaches. Thoughts are made of energy and my ability to perceive energy is a by-product of practicing stillness for over twenty years. In this case, I was able to see the core incident causing her migraines.

I asked the student to sit down and calm her mind while I observed; what I saw resembled a bundle of tightly woven strings within her brain. I asked her if she could feel where the pain was located, and she said she could. I then asked her to direct her conscious awareness close to the pain but not to go in it. In a matter of seconds I saw a scene of her at three or four years of age backed up against the wall in a kitchen and a man yelling at her. As I told her what I was seeing, she said, "I distinctly remember this, that was my dad! Over the years I've never forgotten that incident and I could not understand why he was so mad at me; I was so lovable!" As she began to recall more about the event, I could see the strings of disharmony literally loosening as the pain dissolved, until the headache was gone. Her internalization of her father's anger manifested itself as an electrochemical ball of tension, resulting in headaches. That was a few years ago, and her migraines have not returned.

This is a case when an individual's emotional reaction to an experience at a young age manifested itself over time as an actual physical problem. The next time you get ready to yell at someone, think about what you may be installing in that person's mind. Your thoughts and words are more powerful than you think!

*Negative thoughts
are energy-draining emotions
that not only influence you
but everyone who crosses your pathway.*

Negative emotions carry far more significance than you may realize, and affect people in ways that may surprise you.

Have you walked into a room, made contact with someone who was in a bad mood, and noticed your disposition was influenced? Another's resistant energy can disturb you; causing your own energy level to drop.

People who are negative temporarily become energy vampires literally sucking the life force from those around them. One physical way to detect people with leechlike characteristics, other than the dark cloud that proceeds them, is a drop in your body temperature when you're in their presence. Usually you will notice this phenomenon in your hands, extending into your body, depending on the severity of their negativity and your sensitivity. Energy vampires are very manipulative and can steal your energy without you even knowing it. All you know is that you feel drained being around them.

How do you stop others from robbing you of your life force?

Limit your exposure time. If this is not possible, very gently, with loving energy from within, push outward. A harmonious person will not feed negativity. Your nonreactive being is nonstimulating; consequently, they become disinterested and move away. This technique takes conscious effort to master, but better you control your vibration than forfeit your vitality to another.

Will of mind
is an endowment of the soul,
sustaining you
on your journey of self-exploration.

Will of mind is the governing force of accomplishments and yet few people take the time to understand what motivates them.

Will of mind, or will power, is a basic form of energy. We all know people who are strong-willed, weak-willed, or those who have no willpower at all. Each form of willpower must be directed positively or problems occur.

For example, let's take someone we consider to be strong-willed. This type of person will work toward a goal no matter how much energy is required. But if strong will acts without regard to its impact on oneself or others, it becomes destructive. When strong will escalates out of control, conscious awareness diminishes and the difference between right and wrong is clouded, because excessive amounts of energy override the subtle knowing from deep within.

The QM Practice moderates strong will, strengthens weak will, and empowers no will, activating the calm intuitive consciousness found deep within everyone and known as your true spiritual nature.

Conscious will of mind is fundamentally important if you are to persevere in the practice of meditation. It is an endowment of our soul and ultimately the energy that supports you on your self-exploration.

Ill will
is a sickness of the mind,
with the simple antidote
being stillness from meditation.

Ill will is a sickness within the mind that causes many problems in the world. It is an ignorant, destructive force, directed against oneself or, in hostility, against another.

To understand one's actions, one must understand one's thoughts. Ill will occurs when people are unaware of their thoughts and have lost touch with their conscience. When we cannot feel our conscience, we act without regard for right or wrong, not caring who we hurt along the way. When an individual has suppressed his conscience and defends his damaging actions as right regardless of the cost to himself or others, ill will escalates into malevolence.

To find your conscience, you must begin cultivating a calm will of mind. Silence within your mind diffuses ill will and allows you to trust yourself.

Initially, The QM Practice requires willpower, which is directed from self-concern and reinforced by sitting down and doing The Practice. It will take diligence and discipline to quiet your mind. It may feel as if you are moving against a flow of energy; this is the resistance from your uncontrolled self and the cause of your adversities.

The antidote to ill will is meditation; stillness is like a spiritual salve, eliminating all unwanted irritants. The cure to healing your disorders must begin within you. When you realize you can choose between ill will and health, the choice is clear.

*Behavioral justification
is the perpetuation of ignorance
and a great darkness
across the expanse of mankind.*

Behavioral justification is an internal wall of resistance, protecting what individuals are afraid to look at within themselves. Out of fear, these individuals force, or strongly influence, others into following their belief systems. If everyone else agrees with them, they can believe it themselves. People who intimidate others appear to be externally powerful, but it is a facade; within, they are afraid of their own darkness. The only way to draw attention away from their fear is to project a self-created sense of power onto others.

Justification is a self-created reality which must be validated by others, usually through control issues. If you have to justify your actions, there is an underlying insecurity sending a message that *I am inferior. I am unworthy, so I must rationalize what I do.*

Freedom from fear begins when you drop your guard and face the greatest intimidator of your life—yourself. Anyone can do absolutely anything as long as it does not interfere with another. Is this not enough leeway to explore and enjoy life?

If what you do brings about a harmonious result, you will never have to justify why you do anything. A loving way of life never needs to be defended.

Your mind, in many ways,
is like an elaborate weather pattern
embodying high- and low-pressure systems,
with your thoughts governing the climate.

The thoughts we think and feel govern the weather of our mind, or in other words, our moods. How's the weather in your mind been lately?

A low-pressure system in your mind occurs when you are fearful, angry, depressed, or experiencing stormy times. You will feel dark, gloomy or cold, with your outlook on life the same. When your mind is clouded with negative thought patterns, self-generated thunderstorms of thought activity form, and spin out of control like a cyclone. The more frantic you become, the worse the storm gets.

How do you stop a storm of thought from turning into a full-blown hurricane? By slowing the winds of movement, by quieting your thoughts. When you learn to consciously stop feeding the whirlwind of activity in your mind, spinning thoughts will lose energy and decrease. Sit still and do nothing; with time the tempest will calm to tranquil skies.

When you are in the midst of a high-pressure system, you will feel sunny, clear, and warm. Your mind is calm, collected, and under control; all is serene and peaceful.

When your thoughts flow effortlessly in harmony, the winds of time caress and stir wonder in your soul as you stroll in a world you are glad to be a part of. The weather within regulates your perception of the climate around you, so even if the exterior weather is bleak, you still smile inside. When your true nature is allowed to shine, beautiful days prevail. Everyone will experience storms in their life, but when one blows in your direction, take a look inside at your mental barometer. Your own internal weather system has something to teach you.

Appreciation
is a precious ability of the mind
expressed by an individual
who has released himself from indifference.

Far too often people expend too much time in a fearful form of existence and not enough time experiencing the subtle beauty of life. A daisy is nature's gift, its presence in a field can be captivating if your eyes are open to appreciate it. When you gaze upon a flower and feel indifferent, your mind is pre-occupied, your thoughts are somewhere else. But if you smile at the flower and enjoy its beauty, your soul connects with the flower and a oneness is realized. Because of the many distractions in life, the small flower is often overlooked, overshadowed by what many perceive to be more important.

What can be more important than the well-being of your soul and the appreciation of life that surrounds you?

The next time you are out walking in the world and spot something beautiful in nature, take a moment to share it with a friend. Savor the relationship between your true nature and the nature of the world, and gratitude inside of you will deepen. Appreciation is not a grand affair; it can be the smallest of observations, but of the utmost purity.

Before all else, you must appreciate yourself. You are worthy of it. Only when you recognize the treasure you are—when you discover the magnificence of the true nature of your being—will you be able to perceive the splendor of the world around you.

Endeavor on your travels to find the *joie de vivre*—the joy of living. Indifference is a dimness obscuring the precious nature of life. The true beauty of life is more awesome than you can conceive. Imagine what you cannot imagine, and life can be better than that.

*Wonder is a childlike expression,
from the timelessness of our essence,
knowing no age, bounds, or limitations.*

Wondering about one's essence is the way to open the door to one's self. Wonder is the free spirit of thought, unregulated by linear time or the constraints of a closed mind. Stand in awe of the wonder of your being and allow your mind to absorb the marvels your awareness can perceive.

To reveal their curious nature, each individual must face that which obstructs their ability to explore. When the mind becomes cluttered with complexity, the capacity to perceive wonderment diminishes. Realizing that you must **simply be** is the key to unlocking the miracle of wonder. As Jesus said, "To enter the kingdom of heaven one must become as a small child." A child embraces his true nature. A child can only be a child because he knows nothing else. His soul has not been tainted; he simply is, and thus his mind is free to wonder.

If your intellect blocks your ability to wonder as you become an adult, which way is your mind growing? Is it growing at all?

What sparks your curiosity and why do you not explore it?

What usually restrains fascination is apprehension and cynicism fueled by negative patterns. Most people hold back because they do not know how to release their fears. The QM Practice will train your conscious awareness so you will realize that yielding to fear weakens, and eventually dissolves, the barriers to wonder.

Everyone's essence is a natural marvel, only concealed by a mind that has done nothing to reveal it. Wonder is a gentle impetus which leads you to discover your true nature. The comprehension of the universe within your own mind is the most complete wonder you will ever find. The challenge is to learn, and to enjoy your journey, as each amazement in your life unfolds into the next.

*The gloomy areas of your mind
are only the darkness of unknowing.
Face your fear
with calmness and courage
and darkness will change
into the light of awareness.*

Three

How Do Your Fears Affect You?

*When people
no longer have to fear other people,
mankind will evolve
from an animal to a more spiritual nature.*

If you look at the behavior of humans as a whole, there are still many people who act more like animals than humans. Our planet is plagued with people who continue to feel the need to hurt others.

From the beginning of our evolution as a species, fear has kept us alive. Fear in its most basic form is our instinctive drive for self-preservation. It is fear that activates the release of adrenaline into your system if needed for the fight-or-flight syndrome. Adrenaline supplies the body with short intense bursts of energy, but it is difficult to control. Adrenaline must not rule you or you will be crippled by it. If you have ever been in a confrontation, you will know how hard adrenaline is to control. You usually end up doing things you regret because you act from impulse instead of reason. Adrenaline speeds up bodily functions and is an intense high which some people seem to enjoy, but only at great expense. If you live for this high, you will age before your time and shorten your life span.

Learn to calm your mind, not speed it up! The silent miracle is not experienced when your heart is beating so fast you cannot sit still long enough to enjoy your life. There is a much more beautiful way to live than constantly testing fate.

If you do The Quiescence Meditation Practice, one day in a quiet moment you will experience a silent miracle; you will understand what it is like to really be free of fear and feel your true spiritual nature.

*The shadow of fear
is an ominous dark cloud
often obscuring the well-being
we so desperately seek.*

Living in fear is like being trapped in the dark. Here's an example: I have a student who, for as long as she could remember, had a fear of knives, but she did not know why. One day, as I was observing her meditation, I saw an image of a knife in her mind and asked her what its significance might be to her. She explained that she'd always been afraid of getting cut by a knife. I asked her to quiet her mind; it was then that I saw a thought-form image of a little girl and a young boy standing on a sidewalk. All of a sudden the boy began waving a knife at the little girl, who immediately became frightened. As I was describing the image to my student, she instantly recalled the event, saying, "Oh, that was my cousin! I remember him waving a butcher knife at me and I was terrified he'd cut me!" At that moment her conscious mind observed the scene with the wisdom of an adult and realized there was no longer any threat. By doing The QM Practice, she focused her conscious awareness close to the emotional button, allowed her mind to become still, and in a short time was able to let go of her fear.

The traumas from our past can take a heavy toll on our lives, with or without our knowing it. It is most unfortunate when you do not know how to release yourself from the chains that bind you. Upgrade your well-being. Your wellness is in your own hands, not in the hands of some unknown fear.

*How often are you plagued by
haunting memories from your past,
anxiety about situations in your present,
or persistent apprehensions
about your future?*

Many people hope good fortune will come their way, but out of fear they hold back, or build protective, self-created realities that limit their ability to make their dreams come true. Fear prevents them from achieving their full potential.

The fear from your past cannot hurt you; it is defunct fear! Many times fear from the past may seem real and menacing, but the roots of apprehension are based in a previous experience. Fear from the past has a tendency to repeat itself in endless cycles; a fear that was internalized years ago may come to the surface of your mind countless times until you learn how to dissolve it once and for all.

Present fear is the only fear that can be life threatening and all it's saying is *be careful*. If you are in actual physical danger, distance yourself from the trouble as quickly as possible. This is the only time fear is appropriate. Follow your instinct and respond to the fight-or-flight message telling you it is necessary to take steps to ensure your own safety. Present fear is all about self-preservation. Pay attention.

Fears having to do with the future are groundless. Be mindful of today and you will deal with future events when they occur. You can participate in life only if you are living in each and every moment.

Dwell not on a past, forever frozen in time. And dwell not on the future, which is nothing more than speculation. Examine the moment you are in right now. This is the only moment in time when you can face your fear and do something about it.

*A man
who does not face his fears
is only a shadow of a man.*

It is wise to pay attention to your inner voice when you have a bad feeling about someone or a situation; it is an early-warning system. I often remind students to use their awareness like a scanner on alert for undesirable vibrations. Sensitivity can be used as a powerful tool for self-preservation when facing danger.

Pay attention to warranted fears from dangerous situations that your inner voice is cautioning you about, but also remember not to deny your unwarranted internal fears or to ignore their message: these harmful feelings, if unheeded, eventually command your conscious awareness and become irrational fear, which is the most destructive man-made energy on the planet.

How long will it take before mankind realizes that internal fears are a weakness?

Fears seize and imprison, casting menacing shadows, inhibiting self-expression. When you find one of your own internal shadows, face it but do not attack it, because you will only give it strength. Domination is an illusion. Do not become like a lion tamer with your fears. Brandishing a whip and chair to control what you are uncomfortable with inside of yourself will not permit you to relax. An aggressive stance of coping with your fears will only make you defensive. Let the lion out of the cage. Relax! Soften your vibration and the ferocious cat will quietly walk away. The battle is ultimately won without a fight.

Finding your way out of shady internal corridors calls for fortitude and patience. Scary thoughts of a time gone by are only images of gloomy memories that will continue to haunt you until you decide to take action. Attempting to quiet your runaway thoughts is a courageous exercise. Addressing and dispelling your own shadows is the mark of an adept student.

*Memories from the past
shape the character
of our soul today.*

All of the moments from our past form who we are. If we have had joyous experiences, we are happy most of the time and freer to express who we are without fear. Our loving memories build security within us, helping to form the character of our soul.

If we have had negative experiences, we will experience resistance to life. Resistance shows up in thoughts that have negative emotions attached to them. Our mind is constantly reaccessing these memories, and when this happens unpleasant thoughts and emotions arise. When a painful emotion surfaces, you are limited in your ability to live a harmonious life. Each time a distressing memory wells up, the quality of your life plummets until the emotion contains itself. You literally lose control of your life until the emotion is gone and you regain conscious control. When your mind calms, you can resume your life. But for how long?

The clock of your life is ticking and you are the only one who can make use of each second. The second hand connects each minute to each hour into each day, becoming the expression of your soul. The pathway to understanding your soul lies in each step along the road. Each step represents a mental point in time, with your conscious awareness delineating how you feel about yourself—good or bad. The length of one's life matters not; ultimately it is the quality of comprehension in each second that means everything.

There are those who are young and able to glimpse the eternal, and there are those who are old who can see nothing. The true nature of mind within everyone is timeless.

*When you cannot, will not, or do not
know how to face your fears,
you are powerless to unveil
the nature of your well-being.*

If you do not think fear within affects you, you are deluded. Sooner or later we all must grow up and face our internal demons or else live in the shadows of fear.

Without knowing any better, people put up walls to protect themselves from their fears. These walls are erected so that emotional pain is not felt, but instead of protecting us, these walls imprison us.

When you are in denial of your true feelings, you rationalize your actions. When you use the intellect to justify your actions, you lose the ability to feel from your heart, which is the link to your true nature. Continual justification becomes the perpetuation of ignorance and you become a self-contained dysfunction. You lose touch with yourself and your ability to feel your soul. You become powerless to unmask the dysfunction disguising your well-being.

When you cannot feel your heart, how alive are you?

When you unveil your fears with your conscious awareness, they will vanish. When fears no longer occupy the majority of your mind, you will begin to feel what you have been yearning for: a union with your soul, your true spiritual nature, and the nature of all things.

Delusion
is a pathway leading into darkness;
a person who believes completely
in his delusions
will lose touch with reality.

Delusion is a pathway of self-deception that leads into a dark mental maze of unknowing. Its darkness swallows consciousness, making reality imperceptible. Total truthfulness with oneself is never easy. It takes courage to face your own dark thoughts, and they will be conquered only with a strong ally— your true spiritual nature.

Delusion, in the worst-case scenario, breeds a mind that is totally out of control. This is how the concept of the devil was born and has remained on our planet in the minds of those who do not know the difference between their own genuine thoughts and a runaway, fearful imagination. The supposed existence of the devil was used to explain irrational fears imprisoning an individual within the walls of his own mind. Two thousand years ago Jesus could not have used the terminology, "You have a psychological disorder," because psychology, as we know it today, had not been born.

Delusion can be a very real hell in the minds of those who cannot see their way clear, because delusion consumes and confuses all it touches. This darkness spreading over an individual's mind creates distorted thoughts and alters the perception of reality. When you blindly follow false beliefs and are resistant to reason regardless of the consequences, bad only turns into worse. Senseless irrationality is passed as a mental disease from one person to another. Paranoia can be cured only if you trust in yourself and allow the curative powers of stillness to heal your ignorance. Stop giving energy to the creation of darkness and it will dissolve in the light of awareness.

*Quiet your mind
and the light of awareness
will dispel the darkness of denial.*

Denial is a deep darkness that inflicts pain and suffering wherever present. It can be dispelled only by the awareness born of a quiet receptive mind. Knowing you have problems in your life is the first step to healing denial; without recognizing your plight, you cannot begin rehabilitation.

Those who are in denial are always trying to change others' lives to bring some sense of control to their own. Manipulation and control issues become a way of being: Denial surrounds the individual like a bad odor that everyone smells but them. People who are in denial and unaware of their own controlling behavior mentally stink. There is no nice way to tell someone that the way they treat others is foul. If you run across someone who thinks life stinks, it is because *they* do! If you must be in frequent contact with someone who thinks in this manner, do not mentally rub up against them. If they are open and it is appropriate, educate them about their offensive behavior. You can be sure many others will thank you.

Ignorance of their thoughts and actions is the reason why people are foul and pollute the world. If your own mind is contaminated with ignorance and denial, you will know no different. There are many people who are spiritually illiterate: They do not know how to read and understand their own thoughts.

Denial hides in unaware, self-justified thought patterns that hinder an accurate perception of reality. Clear the clouds of denial with quiet time each day and clarity will reveal self-awareness as surely as the sun dawns each morning.

*Inflicting emotional trauma on another
shows a disregard for human life
and is a regret in the making.*

Inflicting emotional pain on another human being shows a disregard for life and the way emotional buttons are installed in one person by another. One's detrimental behavior can have far-reaching effects on people for many years to come. When someone, with their words or actions, pushes on your resistance, your emotional discomfort—in the absence of an independent conscious awareness—is all-consuming, making it impossible to think rationally. The most common immediate reaction is to lash out and abuse those who triggered your reaction, making them hurt as you do. You may find yourself very close to doing something you may regret. Remember, regrets are sealed in time forever.

How you react when a button is pressed determines whether or not you will be sorry for your actions. How often in the heat of a moment have you done something you can never take back?

If someone traumatizes you, they are acting from their own emotional pain. The problem is theirs. Take not inside what is not yours. When you fully understand this, it will set you free!

But how do you control yourself if you feel a button being pressed? The simplest way to divert someone away from your buttons is to change the subject, but do not mentally avoid your own internal resistance. If you find yourself becoming overly emotional, the wisest course of action is to walk away and give yourself some time to calm down, until you can think rationally. This you will never regret!

*A volatile temper
is an outburst of rage
waiting to explode.*

Volatile tempers create trouble everywhere they explode. To justify rage as a normal part of human function is ignorant. It is so easy to say, "I have a short fuse," and leave it at that. But that's as ludicrous as saying, "It's okay to beat someone up."

Anger is compressed fear made into a human bomb of negative emotion. The psychological damage to those in the vicinity is far-reaching and lasts a lifetime. Anger creates problems everywhere it surfaces, and in some cases installs new buttons in innocent people. An explosive personality tends to put everyone on edge, negatively affecting the lives of others.

For most people, their only way of dealing with their fury is to suppress it, which is like putting a lid on a faulty pressure cooker. Eventually they cannot contain their temper and explode. Typically this is a never-ending cycle.

Usually people with dysfunction are unwilling to face their issues, so they stuff them. They do not realize that what they are avoiding is the very thing they need to look at in order to end their misery. Part of the reason individuals develop avoidance issues is that they do not know how to release their pain and fear has seized their mind.

When you feel yourself getting warm with the rising tide of angry emotion, be on guard with your conscious awareness. It is from mindfulness that the beginning stages of diffusion can occur. The solution to diffusing a hot temper is in practicing stillness of mind. Stillness brightens your light of awareness, illuminating the situation while shutting down the power of negative emotion. Stillness dissolves the wall protecting the temper, and eventually the fear at the core of the problem. When even one temper has been disarmed, the world has just become a safer place to live.

*Avoidance tactics are self-created walls
protecting one's conscious awareness
from the very dysfunction
one needs to release.*

Avoidance tactics take massive amounts of energy to feed and give nothing in return but continued dysfunction. If you become accustomed to avoidance tactics, the original problem is forgotten but still continues to operate, influencing your life without you even knowing it. If you deny your aversions, you are avoiding your avoidance issues. If avoidance issues have more strength than your conscious awareness, your mental capacity is diminished and your ability to reason is compromised. You become illogical!

How do you interact with someone whose avoidance techniques are so strong they are in a state of denial?

If you try to force someone to acknowledge their illogical position, your forceful attitude only strengthens their resistance. Use patience. Watch for a window of opportunity to subtly enlighten them and very gently point out *your* perspective of their problem. Give the individual an opportunity to see what they are doing for themselves without pushing your position on them. If you **need** to prove yourself right, *you* have a problem.

As you dissolve your avoidance issues through The QM Practice, an interesting thing happens; you begin to see the problems of others more clearly because you are not immersed in your own. True spiritual understanding can happen anywhere and to anyone who is open to seeing clearly. It is not forced on anyone; it is shared by one who has nothing to gain but a loving exchange of energy.

*True mental strength
is found in people
who confront internal adversity,
not in those who avoid it.*

The most challenging adversary you will come up against is the fear within you. Avoiding fear will never give you the opportunity to experience the true strength of your mind. Controlling or suppressing fears is not healthy. Avoiding fear does not produce strength in the mind, it weakens it. At this level, adversity wins and you fail.

Blocking out fear is not the same as detaching from it. The blocking of anything within the mind is a wall of resistance feeding disharmony. When you stop trying to control fear, you will have authority over it. When you are not attached to fear, you are not subject to it.

Leave fear alone and you will not sustain it. It will consume itself, instead of you.

As simple as it is, doing The QM Practice releases negativity. A single still point of awareness within breaks the mental ties to your emotional buttons, untangling complexity and weakening negative patterns until the fears simply disappear.

When you *really* let go of a problem from deep within, you will never have to deal with it again! You will be amazed to watch your own reaction when a button of fear is pressed and no emotion comes to the surface of your mind. You will say, "This is a miracle!"

If you could let go of a deep fear you have had for your whole life, would you not call it a miracle?

You can perform this miracle; it can be learned through The Quiescence Meditation Practice.

Worries are like whirlwinds:
they drain energy from your mind
while weakening your immune system.

Worries are like whirlwinds of thought activity, seemingly with a mind of their own, distracting and robbing you of precious time. They are negative energy patterns within your mind. Worry, at its core, is fear and uncontrolled thought drawing the life out of you while perpetuating itself.

What worthwhile endeavor ever came from uncontrolled thoughts?

To think that worry will help you is foolish; a self-defeating program helps no one. Worry is a hesitation interrupting a course of action; it is uncertain thinking, it is not doing and it is certainly not being. Unnecessary worry is a whirlwind going nowhere.

Worries generate disharmonious energy and do not solve anything. To solve a problem one must first have clarity of mind. Allow the winds of worry to die down. When you are overly concerned, take a moment and gaze off at the horizon; your seemingly big obstacle will be put in a clearer perspective. Dissolve mental programs with calm conscious action and the whirlwinds of worry will cease to generate disruption.

To squelch your worry, you must do something about it. The QM Practice teaches the means to break down the confusion by undoing dysfunction with conscious detachment. Learning detachment is a by-product of The Practice. It is a result of allowing your conscious awareness to be still within. Detachment transpires over time—a process that aids in decreasing worries naturally.

We are all a result of our past,
but we do not have
to be held captive by it.

Many people only live by what they know from their past. While we are a product of our past, it does not have to restrict our capabilities or potential.

How do you rise above and cross the boundaries of your limitations? By learning how to detach mind function from brain function. Learn to feel your conscious awareness in each individual second, in each moment, free from the bonds of repetitive thought. Learn to take your thinking off autopilot mode into the independent awareness of mindfulness.

The QM way to attain mindfulness is to drop part of your conscious awareness into your heart area, and simply feel your heart with your conscious mind. This allows your intellect to be observed by an independent conscious awareness associated with your spiritual essence. This is a natural way to bring your consciousness back to mindfulness.

Have you ever done something and when you were finished could not remember doing it?

Many people do this while driving their car; they get to their destination and do not remember the drive. This is dangerous and the reason so many accidents are caused. When you are in autopilot mode, your brain is going through the motions without an awareness of what you are really doing. Your conscious awareness does not have a chance to enjoy the ride because it is somewhere else. Your brain operates your body, collects and shuffles data, but it is not an observant operator. When brain function is the vehicle and a mindful conscious awareness is the driver, your ride in life will not only be smooth, but scenic and enjoyable.

*Endeavoring to find yourself
while standing in the shadow
of fear is frightening;
step out of your fearful existence
into the true nature of God.*

Everyone's true nature of being is, to some degree, hidden behind walls of fear. Most people will not confront fear unless they have to or are forced to.

Have you ever noticed that when an experience you feared is over, you are always glad you confronted your fear and grew from the experience?

Within each individual are varying degrees of light and darkness. The brightness is your own harmonious self-expression and your connection to all that is good and beautiful. The light of awareness brings joyous experience to life and is an expression of God. You have the choice to dwell in the light, to step into the nature of God. Remember, where you stand in your life is controlled by you at all times.

The idea that God should be feared comes from the darkness of failing to understand love. Your loving self-expression is felt from your own heart and is your connection with God. You cannot live and not have the experience of God be a part of you. What is not a manifestation of love, is not a manifestation of life, but a struggle to exist. Anything that is not an expression of love is an expression of death; it is a slowly dying soul. Fear and ignorance are what traps people in a shallow existence and keeps them out of the nature of God.

Within your own hands are all the tools you need to understand light and darkness. We all have tools to brighten our light and it is our own fault if we do not use them. Let go of the darkness of a cold heart and allow the warm, soft glow of love to prevail. When you stop rejecting yourself, you will stop rejecting love. There is only one sacred expression on the planet and it is the expression of love.

*The QM Practice
of stilling the mind
is a natural psychological cleanser.*

With the right practice and patience, all psychological trauma can be released by learning how to drop the walls of resistance that hold emotional wounds in place. Everyone can overcome huge obstacles in their mind, if they know how. What stops most people from trying is *fear*! By adopting ego-boosting techniques, coping mechanisms, and elaborate blocks, many people do not even recognize their dysfunction because they have gotten comfortable with being uncomfortable. A common remark people make when beginning this practice is, "I thought I dealt with this fear already!" They have. They blocked it out so nicely they forget it was there.

It is interesting to note that most people take time to bathe their physical body but do not even consider cleansing what runs their entire life. Begin today, by learning to disinfect your mind of the garbage that has accumulated over the years. Through the simple act of stilling your mind, a great psychological liberation can occur. The calmness of a still mind will diffuse any complex negative emotions and allow normal, healthy functioning to take place. Stillness of mind erases some of the most complex mind dysfunctions imaginable, and you do not have to join a club or leave your home to bring about the change. This form of meditation works miracles. It is a combination of knowing what to do, having the courage to face yourself, patience, and much hard work.

If you could actually release a single fear and know it would never come back, how much would it be worth to you?

Can you envision what it would be like? You cannot; it feels too good to imagine.

*Open your mind
to the landscape of your soul
and you are on a pathway
to finding the missing pieces
of your personal spiritual puzzle.*

Four

What Does Your Life Teach You?

Life teaches
in two fundamental ways:
intellectual knowledge
from the outside world
and self-knowledge
from awareness of one's inner world.

Intellectual knowledge is taught, for the most part, through memorization followed by application. This method is crucial to exchanging and understanding information about our physical world. But does intellectual knowledge alone bring contentment, or does fulfillment come from somewhere else?

In our society, we are most often taught what to think, but not necessarily how to think. The inner workings of how we think, and especially how we feel, are secondary to the expectations and demands of the outside world. If you put self-understanding second, what you give to the world is seconds.

What drives you in your search for self-knowledge? Is it love or is it fear?

Open your spiritual eyes wide! Observe what understanding can be gleaned from darkness. Know that the compartments of fear within your mind are dark only because you are afraid to explore your soul. The light of awareness is the solution to finding contentment and understanding that we are all *all right*. The fear that something is fundamentally wrong with our essence is a delusion. We are all destined for love. Understanding our true spiritual loving nature through self-exploration is the way to heal our souls and then the planet.

The QM Practice calms the mind so the expression from your heart to the outside world can be of the purest quality. When your mind is clear, you gain the freedom to choose your destiny, and thus the expression of your soul will become obvious; it will be love.

*What everyone
needs to know
is what they do not understand
about themselves.*

Intellectual knowledge is a good first step to understanding yourself, but what about a recurring personality problem?

How do you study a part of yourself that human eyes cannot see?

How often have you observed a friend or relative behaving badly and they are not aware of their dysfunction?

Have you ever thought that you could be suffering in the same manner?

To really start a pathway of self-discovery, you must first admit you are unenlightened about yourself. As you begin practicing Quiescence Meditation, your conscious awareness relaxes and you gain sensitivity through the cultivation of calm mental energy. You begin sensing subtle, deeper realms within that are difficult to detect with a distracted mind. Learning to consciously focus on subtle inner changes trains your awareness to function like a microscope, seeing deeper into the inner space of your being. When you become attuned to subtlety, negative energy-draining patterns become clear and are allowed to dissipate. Without the distraction of deeply rooted problems, your conscious awareness is free to explore the inner workings of your being.

What everyone needs to do is to consciously stop fighting with their mind and work with it. A tranquil mind is a jewel in the universe and can be appreciated only by one who has learned its value.

Is your mind a worthless piece of junk or a finely polished jewel?

Polish your mind by bringing your awareness to a still point within and you will learn what you do not know about yourself.

*Acknowledging the difference
between what you know
and what you do not
is like understanding the difference
between abundance and destitution.*

The desire to plant a tree is a noble task, but without the knowledge or sufficient care to plant correctly, the tree may wither and die. We are very much like trees, requiring care and attention. When we are young, care from our parents is vitally important so we are grounded properly; but as we grow to maturity, the responsibility to support ourselves becomes our own. Ultimately, we cannot depend on any other person for that which is necessary to sustain our soul. Each one of us is responsible for his own soul. Only when you have nurtured your own soul and cultivated abundant harmony within will you have enough to give to another.

If you are not an example of spiritual bounty, what do you have to give to another?

Cultivating self-awareness is of the utmost importance if you are to grow and flourish. Without self-love, the soul thirsts; spiritual dehydration will push you into a downward spiral toward destitution. But all that is needed to pick yourself up is to care for your being. A gentle thought of kindness will do wonders for your soul. But you must find the source of your well-being; you must find your spiritual well and then drink from it. The source of your well-being is within you already. Your true spiritual nature is the water; it is waiting for you to quench your thirst. Recognizing what you know about your spiritual well and what you do not, is the difference between abundance and destitution.

*The emergence of self-expression
is the dawning of individual contentment
on a pathway destined to happiness.*

For everyone, the ability to express their distinctive character begins in childhood. If a child is nurtured and allowed self-expression by loving parents, a natural, healthy growth to adulthood is the result. Balance between the thinking and feeling processes develops, manifesting a foundation of security, acceptance, and confidence. Parents pass love to their children, permitting the youngsters' creativity to develop. Positive reinforcement encourages individuality, and a child learns to have fun without needing approval from others, while the inner glow of a youthful true nature begins to shine.

On the other hand, negative reinforcement forces children to protect themselves and put up walls. When a parent demeans a child's self-expression, inhibitions form, mutating into unhappiness and dysfunction. A demoralized youngster acts out by looking for trouble, and counterproductive patterns become deeply ingrained. If the only way a child receives attention is through misbehaving, trouble will follow like a shadow. Delinquency develops into unconscious behavior. The more a parent tries to change and control an unruly kid, the stronger his resistance becomes. When troubled teenagers become adults, their walls will not allow them to establish intimacy. If they marry and have children, the cycle continues.

An often-neglected secret to happiness is learning to be open to your own self-expression. The QM Practice teaches you to fear not the beauty of your self-expression; it is the blossoming of your soul.

*Our soul's mission
is to learn how to free ourselves
from our own difficulty.*

The morning arrives and your eyes open to a new day. Thoughts within your mind begin to surface, but from where do they originate?

The outside world is the soul's playground and touches places in our memories, evoking feelings that influence our day. Whether our memories are happy or sad is determined by our conscious perception at the time of origin. If we react to a situation negatively and file the memory in our brain network, headaches occur. If we take this same circumstance to heart, heartaches occur. Whether we internalize a negative experience mentally or emotionally, we allow pain into our being and an electrochemical button or point of resistance forms. Now we must protect ourselves by separating the unpleasant memory from our conscious awareness; we do this by creating compartmentalized dysfunction in our mind. The situation worsens when we put up a wall of mental energy to distance ourselves from the internal negativity.

When our conscious awareness merges with dysfunctional thought patterns, our ability to perceive the here and now is interrupted. The interruptions become hesitation and we are frustrated by unwanted distracting images. Fear-based patterns drive conscious awareness, and if enough time elapses, the mind adjusts to them. The smooth operation of our minds is hindered by walls, doubts, and fears that distract, impinge on, and surround our conscious awareness.

The pathway of awareness unfolds moment by moment; gloomy recollections of past pain keep you from experiencing the present and hinder your journey. The darkness of dysfunction is a cancer in the mind; it is slow, painful agony. When negative programs are dissolved through The QM Practice, everyone can free themselves from their own difficulty and enjoy life.

*Knowing you have a problem
does not necessarily mean
you will let go of it.*

The first step to releasing a problem is recognizing you have one. However, you may know full well you have a problem and yet still be unable to get rid of it. Knowing you have an issue that needs to be addressed is a step in the right direction, but it is not enough. Letting go of a problem with the intellect can work, but is limiting because most psychological problems are protected with walls of resistance or elaborate complex blocks that the brain cannot overcome. You may think you've eradicated an issue, but you may be deluding yourself, or the problem is so securely protected you may not even be aware that it's there.

I've had numerous students come to me after a few months of doing The Practice and exclaim, "I thought I worked this problem out already!" My response is, "If an issue continues to come out of your mind, it is still there." Quite frequently I am also asked, "How come I cannot let go of my issues faster?" And I explain, "If your being changes too rapidly, it will spark resistance, because you will not know what you are changing into. Your own fear will only allow you to grow as fast as is comfortable. Also, as you release buttons, it is important to allow your true spiritual nature to fill in the empty space left behind."

In traditional forms of psychotherapy, conscious awareness is strengthened by talking about problems and learning coping techniques to deal with them. This approach helps emotional buttons to vent but does not dissolve and release bound-up mental energy. Talking about problems alleviates pressure but does not douse the fire causing the emotion. The QM Practice is not merely a means of coping; it is a way of extinguishing the blaze that causes negative emotions.

Mentally abusing yourself
while in a painful condition
only makes a bad situation worse!

One of the most common negative behavior traits involves the battle between one's dysfunction and one's conscious awareness. Many times when an individual is confused or cannot see a way around an obstacle, he becomes frustrated and starts to browbeat himself. Beating up on yourself is a demented way of being.

How is abusing yourself going to help anything?

Self-torture actually is a deranged form of self-control. The first step to recovery is awareness. Once you are aware of your condition, you can begin to calm your conscious awareness and be kind to yourself. Self-punishment helps no one and is at the opposite end of the spectrum from your true spiritual nature. Give yourself the only lasting comfort for your soul: allow the true spiritual nature of your being to caress you.

Have you noticed that happiness always correlates to times when you care for and like yourself? Inner kindness forms each time your conscious awareness touches into the direct experience of your heart. The result is a pathway heading toward the salvation of your soul.

There are many skeptics in the world who question whether true redemption of the soul is possible. The source of salvation and purity of thought is not found in the outside world, but realized when the path to your heart and soul is cleared of obstacles. The cleaning process is each individual's obligation.

Are you meeting the responsibility of cleanliness for your soul?

*Whether world events unfold
with toil or effortlessly
depends upon individual awareness.*

The world is a manifestation of collective individual awareness. Only through the effortless energy of our true nature will civilization experience lasting positive change. When we are constantly forcing life to happen, discontentment and frustration are the result. The mind becomes stressed with plans, deadlines and, worries, and we are held hostage by our own refusal to let mental images go. Endeavoring to catch up becomes a pipe dream, but we still keep thinking, "If only I can get this done, then I can rest." But there is always more to do.

How do you end the condition of "never-done-ism"?

Never-done-ism will disappear when you are no longer driven by compulsive patterns. This cannot be intellectualized; it must be learned through another process called *detachment*. To most people, being free within their mind is an unrealistic fantasy or can happen only on vacation, when they can temporarily escape. When your conscious awareness learns to free itself from the need to constantly do, characterized by the intellect, you will run your life instead of your activities running you.

The QM Practice teaches you how to free yourself from your own self-torture. The key is transcending linear time associated with brain function and flowing with the true nature of your being. Allow your essence to be your master and the events of your life will unfold in ways that will startle your intellect. A smooth uninterrupted flow of energy is a beautiful way of being.

If you cannot find this ideal state, who or what is in control of your life?

*Saints and sages of the world
have followed for millennia
an unwritten precept of the universe:
the spiritual law of noninterference.*

Interfering in the lives of others is a collective societal problem and an enormous drain of mental energy, culminating in dissonance. Each time you meddle in the life of another, you set karma (the law of cause and effect) into motion. Negative karma manifests itself externally in the form of civil and criminal laws, and internally as guilt and denial over how one mistreats another.

The spiritual law of noninterference is not only about how we treat others but also about how we treat ourselves. Interference begins and ends within each individual. If you mistreat yourself, you will mistreat others. When each individual becomes mindful of his own life and works out his internal buttons, harmony in our world will develop.

The most important life to transform is your own; it is the only life you have a right to change. Allow others to make their decisions and you will free yourself from a responsibility that was never yours to begin with. When you make choices for someone else, dependency forms, inhibiting growth. Allow others to learn from their mistakes. If someone asks for your assistance and you can help, great. Do so. When you do not intrude in the life of another, you free your soul and allow others to learn their lessons, not yours.

*Permitting mental debilitation
for the sake of a relationship
is a degradation of one's spirit.*

In my early years I dated a woman who would say to me, "If you never say or do such and such, I will never get angry." At first, I agreed to yield to her demands, until more and more issues were added to the list, leaving me mentally incarcerated by her restrictions. Allowing yourself to become mentally imprisoned for the sake of a relationship is a degradation of your spirit, and is bound to cause resentment.

Controlling people manipulate others to bring a sense of order to their own lives. But their domineering behavior is at the expense of others. Those who live or work around an authoritarian pay a price in anxiety because they must tiptoe around dysfunction so as not to feel the wrath of an exploding button. Harassing your fellow human beings is mental weakness and a mark of ignorance.

In a healthy relationship, each party must have free will or animosity will build, leading to an explosive confrontation. Only by dissolving patterns associated with control issues can a relationship grow and prosper. Buttons of resistance and negative emotional conditions need to be treated like an illness. Unfortunately, many people live with their negativity, depression, and feelings of despair, not realizing they are suffering from a form of psychological disease.

Life can be so much easier if you become responsible, through mindful awareness, of your thoughts and actions. Each individual's freedom from dysfunction must be won by his own efforts, or degradation in relationships will continue.

True detachment
is not a separation from life
but the absolute freedom within your mind
to explore living.

True mental detachment is the ability to allow people and circumstances to be who and what they are. Far too many people expend tremendous amounts of energy manipulating or interfering in the lives of others.

Insecurity is the number-one reason people form attachments. When your conscious awareness is tied to a need to please or influence others, you are mentally attached. Attachments within the mind occur on the conscious level, which you are probably aware of; the subconscious level, which you may or may not be aware of; and the unconscious level, which you are totally unaware of.

The way to relinquish mental attachments is not to change the outside world, but to change how you relate to others from within. When you mentally release your need to control, you will free yourself from unnecessary worries and concerns. Attempting to control the world is the act of a deluded mind.

Through The QM Practice you will learn to dissolve programs that force your conscious awareness to cling and attach. As you practice and release compulsive patterns, space within your mind appears, giving you time to contemplate, uninterrupted by controlling thought images. When your soul has developed enough free space to make clear choices without any negative influence, you can consciously live according to your true nature.

Allow the outside world to be what it is and your mind will allow you to be who you are. You cannot imagine the freedom that comes with true detachment. It is an exquisite way to live.

*In a single quiescent moment,
when your mind is free
from the burdens of life,
a miracle can happen,
a missing piece of your spiritual puzzle
can be found.*

Within each of us are blank areas of the soul—unenlightened parts of our essence that are basically missing pieces of our spiritual puzzle. Trying to describe an unrealized part of the soul is like trying to describe a foreign land to someone who has not traveled there. They can only imagine what it's like, but they cannot know!

Missing pieces of your spiritual being are elusive, but when you find one, in the depths of your soul, you know it. Listen to this story: One afternoon, I was standing on our balcony overlooking a sapphire-blue Pacific Ocean. It was a beautiful, clear, sunny day with a gentle breeze. As I admired the view, I noticed a young couple walking across the street. Suddenly a tingling sensation surged through me, and I remember feeling as if I was absorbing the scene instead of merely spectating. While this was happening, a profound thought hit me: *These young people are simply living their lives!* I had never had this particular perception before. The realization connected my conscious awareness to the core of my being and I was aware that something deeply meaningful had transpired. Up until that moment, the basic awareness of simply living my life without pretenses had eluded me. *Life does not need a reason to be, it just is.* Why had I never had this thought before? Perhaps my mind was too busy to experience what was really important. I now find I have a finer appreciation of life.

When you reach a state of placidity, your conscious awareness will be in the optimum state to attain what you are *really* here to do: find and fill in the missing pieces of your spiritual puzzle.

The true spiritual lessons of life
manifest themselves
when we are quiet
and at peace with our soul.

Many people dedicate a great deal of time to career goals, but what about personal spiritual fulfillment? What about why you are *really* here?

No one comes into this life aimlessly wandering; everyone has a purpose. Ultimately, your purpose is to find those parts of your soul that you do not understand. When you devote time to understanding your spiritual essence, you begin to experience your individual significance. As you uncover the real you, your self-expression becomes evident and you find yourself exploring new ways of being.

The QM Practice provides an all-encompassing way to free and prepare your conscious awareness to operate, detached from the compartmentalized patterns in your mind. The tranquil atmosphere of empty space within the mind brings receptivity to your conscious awareness and sensitizes you to subtle changes in energy. An ultrareceptive awareness allows you to pause and sense the finer nuances in mindfulness. When the conditions are right, a perceptive awareness fully absorbs an experience, allowing a true spiritual lesson to be realized; filling in a missing piece of your spiritual essence. A new sense of self is achieved and a brand-new mental skill is born, releasing you from the bonds of ignorance. One day, when you are in the right frame of mind, a subtle profound thought will dawn on you and you will experience a thought that is an unmistakable trait of finding a missing piece of your spiritual puzzle. *Why have I never looked at life in this way before?*

Do The QM Practice and you will not have to hunt for the right space; *it* will find *you*. Then you will not have to pursue your life's lessons; you will become them.

*Endow yourself
with time to sit down
for a few minutes each day
and embrace the simple beauty
around you.*

Five

How Do You Experience Time?

Each moment is alive,
not to be captured and held prisoner,
but to be experienced as contentment
by one who understands
the true nature of time.

We have all heard people say, "This moment is the only moment there is," but what does this really mean? The past is gone forever and the future is tenuous conjecture. All we really have is this instant, *right now*! Experience this second as you read these words, this is where you are!

How is this present moment affecting you?

Everyone has had daydreams of what it would be like to live a life that is a continuous flow of beauty and wonder, but why does this not happen? Desires, cravings, and attachments poison our thoughts to the point of making us ill. We wish each moment would pass quickly, hoping another moment will mysteriously bring relief. But the next moment is the same; we are trapped in a self-created toxic pattern. To escape, we divert our attention with outside activities or feebly cling to memories. But this offers no release, it only robs us of the genuine treasure that is found in the eternal moment. We occupy our days with busyness and distractions but still we have to face our mental disorders someday.

The day has arrived. Use The QM Practice to dissolve time-stealing abnormalities once and for all. Stillness of the mind and introspection will break us out of negative thought patterns. Each individual must take the initiative to dispel the darkness of discontent with enlightenment from his true nature, or suffering will only continue.

*If you have too much to do
and not enough day to do it in,
you will age before your time.*

In a life full of duties and responsibilities, it is easy to become hyperactive, going nowhere fast. Many people give themselves a break only when nothing else needs to be done or when they get sick. If you let the outside world dictate your free time, you may find yourself with no free time at all.

Becoming preoccupied in a fast-paced world makes you feel more like a robot than a human. When too many thoughts precede your actions, you are out of sync or out of phase with yourself. When your mind is muddled, you can't feel your true nature. Having two, three, or four thoughts all at the same time leaves you feeling scattered and confused. Out-of-phase living not only affects you, but everyone who crosses your pathway. A hurried demeanor puts everyone on edge; you cast out negative vibrations, leaving those around you feeling irritable and uneasy. If you are out of sync and if you are a parent, you are probably passing your condition on to your children. You are likely sending an unconscious message that it's okay to be rushed and crazed.

Time slips through the hands of an out-of-sync person. When you are too busy running around, trying to do everything, you usually do nothing. You're so preoccupied with what you think you need to accomplish, you don't notice the years pass you by. People who are out of phase usually grow old before their time. Do you know what time it is?

End this mental condition by slowing down and centering your conscious awareness each day. Do not put more into your day than you can realistically handle. Try cutting back on your activities by about fifteen percent and watch how much better you will feel. Give yourself a fifteen percent raise in time.

Time being money, how well do you pay yourself?

*W*hen the mind
is consciously calmed,
stress from hurry and worry
dissolves into insignificance.

Stress from hurry occurs when too many thoughts precede your actions, when what you are thinking about is not what you are doing. This state of mind leaves you feeling behind schedule and floundering. Do not be so hard on yourself. Do not have unrealistic expectations of what can be accomplished. Slow down, calm your mind! Enjoy what you do and stress will not overwhelm you.

If you do feel tense and harried, try this exercise: Close your eyes and with your conscious awareness feel the surface of your mind—a horizontal, electrochemical plane of energy directly at eye level. Now pull all of your conscious awareness together, to a pinpoint of energy at the center of the surface of your mind; this is where mental consciousness is located. Keeping your consciousness centered at the surface of your mind dissipates anxiety because you are focused in the moment instead of in the future. You will notice that when you are focused in the moment, all distractions vanish. Everyone has had the experience of doing a task and being oblivious of everything around them; this state of mind is known as mental consciousness or absorption.

When the outside world requires you to move quickly, move as efficiently as possible while maintaining your conscious awareness at your center. As you learn to work from your center, you can learn to move swiftly with a sense of grace about you. When you enlighten yourself as to why you unknowingly allow yourself to rush, you will learn to go slow, stay centered, and enjoy your life.

*Allocate time
for your personal well-being
or the rigors of daily life
may dominate your schedule.
Grant yourself time to enjoy simplicity.*

It is easy to let the rigors of life get out of hand and leave you with no time for yourself. Scheduling time for lighthearted activities or doing absolutely nothing except being who you are is therapy for the soul.

There was a time when I used to enjoy watching a certain frivolous television program. My wife couldn't quite understand what drew me to this show and questioned my attraction to it. One day I had the opportunity to ask a teacher who is a Tibetan Buddhist master why I was drawn to watch the show. He told me that because I was so serious most of the time, I sometimes needed some humor in the form of mindless stupidity to balance my life.

Find time for levity, even if it may seem silly and totally insignificant. If your responsibilities have been addressed, you are not being lazy, only taking time to relax and detach yourself from the have-to's of life.

Can you grant yourself time to unwind and laugh?

Incorporate time in your day to relax. You will be astonished by how soothing it feels not always to be pushed by yourself or anyone else. Living free from pressure is amazingly simple. Live life, your life! Allow your soul to experience what is, and simply be. Book more free time in your calendar for you and one day you will reflect back and realize your leisure times were actually some of the happiest and best times of all.

*Take care of today
and tomorrow
will take care of itself.*

Have you ever pondered the motion that is produced as each day unfolds into the next? This subtle movement draws our souls into the future; some call it time, others call it aging, and still others just call it change. The direction and quality of this motion is determined by how well you care for yourself. Without genuine concern for the wellness of your soul, you lose the ability to feel contentment.

Without contentment in your daily activities, is there meaningful significance in your life?

If you feel dissatisfied and disregard the importance of today, hoping tomorrow will mysteriously be better, you are neglecting the power of your own mind. You must eventually stop escaping from the aspects of yourself that you do not like, either by your own choice or by a painful circumstance such as physical illness or a mental breakdown. When you are stressed to the point of illness and too weak to run, then you will decide to take care of yourself. Why wait for this to happen?

If you have never cared for yourself, it is time to start. All you have to do is try. Every time you do The QM Practice, you are caring for yourself by giving your conscious awareness time to connect with your heart and soul. Watch carefully; the place where this moment in time meets your conscious awareness, this is the eternal moment and the place where the experience of life truly happens.

Within each moment is the opportunity to experience and fulfill any dream. By neglecting mindfulness, you miss the beauty of this moment. Today is all you have. Tomorrow does not exist! Each day, when you wake, it is today; tomorrow never comes. Take care of yourself today and tomorrow will take care of itself.

*Bygone negative emotions
often taint the present moment,
creating distorted perspectives of time.*

It is quite common for experiences to be twisted out of proportion; becoming more dramatic than they actually were. This is particularly true with children. Misinterpreted perceptions account for many of the dysfunctions that adults live with. Distorted scenes filed in a child's memory as resistant points of electrochemical energy are continually activated, poisoning the present moment.

A surprising change happens as you release these resistant points from your mind: your perception of each individual moment becomes clearer. You find yourself fully absorbing the present, free of the distractions from past negative conditioning. A significant turning point occurs on your spiritual pathway when you begin to experience life as it really is. Your mind opens to a panoramic recognition of nature; you find yourself intimately connected with the sky, the trees, and the birds, as all nature comes alive. Your surroundings reflect a warm feeling, with your true spiritual nature and the environment experienced as one. You feel connected with the natural world and cherish your place in it.

The present is priceless. This moment will never come again. Only when you free your mind from distorted images of the past will you be able to enjoy more meaningful experiences of time. The QM Practice restores your childlike sense of wonder without compromising wisdom.

If you could release yourself from your troubled past, what would it be worth?

You have an opportunity and it is now!

117

*When psychological buttons
no longer consume your mind,
a fascinating phenomenon happens:
time appears seemingly out of nowhere.*

Without training, the mind is subject to becoming a prisoner of the past. You need to know how to flow with and embrace each new moment, independent of old psychological patterns.

When your conscious awareness learns to free itself from repetitive cycles of negative energy, you will find yourself with increased free time because you are no longer consumed by reactive emotion from old memories. Instead of time slipping away as you are preoccupied with the past, you will be able to experience each moment as it happens. As each button of resistance is dissolved, more time appears. It is astounding how many minutes, hours, and days are wasted because our awareness is trapped in closed-loop repetitive patterns.

When you release electrochemical dysfunction, your consciousness yields freedom. When you are fully present in the moment, minutes and hours fluidly cascade into each other; you become so completely involved in the moment that you lose awareness of linear time.

Experiencing uninterrupted periods of simply being in the present allows you to experience a fascinating phenomenon known as *empty mind*. Located deep within, this state of mind allows thinking without the constraints of linear time; it knows only the direct experience of any given event. This state of mind liberates you to explore previously unknown facets of your world and yourself.

When psychological buttons no longer consume your mind, you will simply have more time. Release yourself from thoughts that are not of this moment, and you will learn to command the use of time!

*Hidden within each moment
is a new experience waiting to happen;
but out of insecurity and fear,
many live in a narrow zone of comfort
which, by their own hand,
gradually becomes a self-created prison.*

Hidden within each moment is a new experience waiting to be born, but often newly forming realizations become shrouded by patterns of insecurity. We fear anything new, so in an attempt to control events, we try to mold the situation into something familiar; we try to duplicate a past experience in hopes of re-capturing a feeling we're comfortable with. Clinging to old patterns limits new experiences and inhibits openness.

Deliberately initiate new experiences! Live your life abundantly. Do not attempt to create the condition of living. New thoughts generate new feelings by consciously permitting unexplored adventures to enter your soul.

The struggle to open one's conscious awareness is an age-old problem that has nothing to do with age and everything to do with clarity of mind. The limitation placed on one's mind is not from age, but from what one does with one's mind. All limitations are self-imposed. The mind is timeless and knows no boundaries.

Meditating and contemplating are consciousness-opening exercises. As a person sits and contemplates his life, the experience of mind unfolds. All one needs to do to understand one's self is to look. Look at what you have built in your mind that imprisons you. Just as walls have been built, walls can be taken down. Linear time matters not to the mind, only the experience of what you do with it.

*W*hen intellectual linear time
yields to the true nature of nonlinear time,
a new understanding
of being in the moment emerges.

As thought activity within the brain slows from hyperactivity to calmness, your perception of time begins to change. Time is no longer linear, it is no longer bound to the intellect. Instead, as the mind is stilled and you operate from a peaceful conscious awareness, time exists only as a progression from one moment to the next.

Linear time is like a prison sentence; we lose the freedom to live our lives. We are chained to schedules, agendas, and time lines. We try to run to a future that is forever out of our reach, and we're held back by a past that traps us in a repetitive cycle of negative energy.

Only when we have clarity of mind can we fully appreciate the present. Through a silent miracle, we can disengage the buttons that trigger the resurgence of memories and finally experience the present in all its fullness. Only then, when we live fully in the present, are we capable of expressing our true nature.

No one is more powerful than a person who flows from his true nature. This person is not a captive of time; he just is. Time stands still and he is present and completely mindful in the moment, absorbed in what he is doing. The desire to be in another time or place is not even a remote consideration.

When your intellect yields to the limitless space of your true nature, hurry and worry become distant memories. When the true nature of time transforms our man-made conception of time, a watch changes from a shackle into a bracelet.

Patience is mastery of the moment.
It is the gift of time
to those who can be still long enough
to perceive its value.

There is an old story about a master who was walking down a road with a few of his students. The master stopped by a tree to rest and enjoy the beauty of the day. But his students were so filled with impatience that they could not sit still, so they ran over to the next hill to see what was on the other side. The master shook his head and with a smile said to himself, "Have I taught them nothing? My students still do not know that what they are looking for is right here, not over there. There will be there, when you get there, but there is only one *here*."

As you practice Quiescence Meditation and begin to release your resistance, you will notice that your heart feels lighter and more free. You will also notice a sensation that can be described only as more room or space within; in Buddhism, this state of mind is known as emptiness or nothingness. When you allow your life to unfold naturally, you will understand that this so-called nothingness is actually everything. This form of nothing can be experienced only after much practice and with the patience that comes from the discipline of developing a still mind. This kind of nothing does not mean doing nothing; this kind of nothing translates as the ability to do everything!

*Love costs you nothing to give
but costs you everything
when you cannot.*

Six

How Does Love Grow?

Self-awareness is the path to love;
what blocks this path
is unwarranted fear.

Have you ever wondered how a child's personality is shaped? Anytime a child feels hostility coming from another, his automatic response is to throw up a wall of defense because he knows of no other way to protect himself. Defensive behavior sets up a condition where children learn to close off areas of their mind. When the natural wonder of a child's mind is diminished by the erection of walls of defense, negative emotion is formed in an innocent mind. Negative emotion inhibits a child's self-expression and creates a fear-based way of loving. The individual will remain emotionally deficient unless he learns how to love without fear.

To understand how you perceive love, retrace how your concept of love evolved. Take a close look at how you love your mother and father. Mentally step back and observe how you relate with your parents and you will find the patterns that formed the basis of your relationships in adulthood.

How is a fearful way of existence as an adult transformed into the natural wonder of a child again? The wonder of a child can return to a grown-up through releasing fear and embracing love. Your pathway to love is in understanding your mind.

Explore your heart and soul bravely.

Each time you do The QM Practice the veil of ignorance recedes, revealing why you do what you do. When you are able to recognize how you love and what you fear, you are able to control your own destiny.

*When an open heart
is the first priority in your life,
care will bring forth love.*

The most devastating occurrence that can happen to a young soul is not being cared for. The interaction between parent and child sets the stage for how one perceives love. Care is the first step to love, but for some reason, a caring attitude is not always a priority.

What is wrong with this picture?

If you were raised with kindness, encouragement, and trust, your heart will naturally be open. If you were neglected or abused, and took it personally, your heart closes off, forming a cold disposition. Heartaches become electrochemical bundles of energy that stop many people from feeling love. Negative energy patterns from a harsh and abusive upbringing can produce excruciating emotional pain, closing off the conscious mind to love.

How do you break the constraints of the past and learn to love? First, you must provide yourself with the care you need. You must shower your soul with kindness and treat yourself in a loving manner. But the care for oneself must be coupled with a way to dissolve the detrimental, relentless signals that keep your heart shut. Open your mind to The Quiescence Meditation Practice and you will learn to open your heart to love. The experience of love is already within you; it is the life force of your spirit.

Why do you not seek where your treasure is waiting?

Fear of abandonment
in the mind of a child
is a withdrawal
from the nature of love.

Abandonment issues are rampant in our society. The effects of abandonment are far-reaching and usually manifest as insecurity. Here is an example: There is a student in one of my classes who is every teacher's dream—she listens and does her practice. One day she missed class, the next week she missed again, so I called to see how she was doing. She told me she was afraid—consumed by fear and had no idea why. I reassured her she was processing out an issue and asked her to come to class the following week. A couple of days later she phoned. In an excited voice she told me her fear was gone and she knew what had caused it. She explained how upon completing her meditation practice, a childhood memory ran across her mind. She remembered being a young girl and her father walking out the front door in his navy uniform leaving for sea duty. It was common for her father to be gone for months at a time because of his job, but it was unsettling for her as a child. She loved her father, but each time she would start getting close to him, he would have to travel. In her mind, his leaving created a thought pattern: *If I love someone, they will leave me.* This thought became an unconscious program, compromising her ability to love for about thirty years. The realization and release of the electrochemical program dramatically changed her; she now is free to love without fear of being abandoned.

Can you imagine holding back your love for another because of a misconception?

Your mind has every answer to every question about yourself.

Why do you not contemplate the reasons you have difficulty with love?

*Adolescence
is a state of mind,
and not necessarily a loving state.*

In adolescence, as in all periods of growth, experiences shape the constitution of the soul. How our soul forms during adolescence depends enormously on how love is expressed by those who influence us during this crucial time. If we are shown the freedom that genuine love offers, self-assuredness and confidence form. If we are humiliated and degraded, desperation results, becoming integrated in our sense of self as a negative energy cycle, causing depression and the acting out of dysfunction. In an attempt to take charge of his life, a desperate person will utilize methods such as gossiping, neglecting responsibility, fighting, drug abuse, eating disorders, or becoming an escapist to avoid the outside world.

When an adult becomes angry or reacts as a result of having a button pressed, he reverts to being a child because emotionally he has never grown up. How many adults do you know who behave like juveniles?

The QM Practice will slowly open your memory, retrace your steps, and reveal why particular incidents really happened and how they affect you. If you long to improve emotionally and love without interfering patterns, you must release your unsavory past or every relationship will be a replay of unresolved hurts.

*Only when we truly
understand love
can we actually find it.*

As we mature from adolescence to adulthood, a stirring within occurs. Hormonal changes produce physical attraction to others, resulting in feelings like adulation and infatuation and causing us to indulge in sexual fantasies. The instinctual drive that develops in adolescence has kept our species in existence. But when hormones overrule common sense, the physical expression of love can be quite confusing. It is easy to understand why people have so much difficulty with love: they confuse it with sex.

Is senseless idolizing of another person the cornerstone of genuine caring and tenderness? Adoration and animal magnetism may seem like love, but do they provide a foundation for a pure, long-lasting relationship?

Physical attraction can start a loving relationship, but how does a couple endure difficulties and continue to grow together? When physical beauty and sex become familiar, what remains? Physical appearance means little unless there is heartfelt love within.

The QM Practice teaches how to find the true nature of love within. Love is about harmony; it is about evolving into one's true spiritual nature. Everyone's true spiritual nature is absolute love. The true understanding of love is found in your perception of who you are within.

One day, with much patience and practice, a deep, unstoppable smile will rise up from your heart. The smile will be a reflection of what you see within, and what you will behold is your loving, everlasting essence.

The fear of being alone,
in reality,
is only the absence of understanding
the true nature of love.

The most widespread fear, the one everyone eventually confronts is the fear of being alone. Most people experience this fear when their aloneness is not by their choice and when they are at their weakest—i.e., when they lose a loved one either through a broken relationship or death. The fear of being alone is really the fear of not feeling love. This is terrifying, even to a seemingly stable person.

If you feel inadequate when you are by yourself, it is because you have not mastered self-love. It is natural to be sad when you feel lonely and desolate. Recognizing and addressing areas of your mind that bring forth sorrow call for courage and these areas should be explored bravely. You are not subhuman because you are lonesome. You are just by yourself!

People usually avoid being alone by keeping busy, and yet the only way to truly know yourself without the distractions of activities and responsibilities influencing you, is by finding solitude.

Meditation is the means to master loneliness. Consciously taking time for introspection after your practice is the best way to understand the fear of loneliness.

When you can be alone without feeling lonely, you will learn self-acceptance. Self-approval will grow to contentment, allowing the true nature of self-love to unfold. Within you is the capacity to give and receive love beyond measure; what hinders you is your inability to be alone with yourself.

*Tears dissolve the wall of illusion
between who we pretend to be
and who we really are.*

Throughout my personal spiritual journey, I have shed many a tear. Tears help to wash away the impurities caused by our traumatic thoughts. We cry tears of grief when we're hurting, and tears of joy when we're happy. Our tears urge us to feel ourselves and bridge the gap between who we pretend to be and who we really are. Each time we cry, we are very close to our heart. Do not ever be ashamed to cry; there is something wrong when you cannot cry. If you cannot cry, you cannot really feel your heart.

Many people hold back their tears so as not to experience emotional pain, but in doing so, they block the love that is beneath their wounds. Protecting the heart from pain is a temporary anesthesia, but only prolongs suffering. Holding back your tears desensitizes your heart and weakens your soul. By negating your emotions, you become numb and incapable of feeling.

How alive are you, if you cannot feel?

Heartaches are signs trying to tell you that something is not right. Being aware of heartaches is the start to releasing despair. Relax your conscious awareness in the presence of your hopelessness and you will begin to watch the wall surrounding your heart disappear. Be patient. Emotional hindrances that have been with you for years will take more than a couple of days to release.

When the spiritual water of tears washes away the obstructions to our heart, our soul opens to the nature of our being. Our tears represent a mere few drops from an expanse of love mightier than any ocean. When allowed to flow, tears set forth a trickle that finally merges with the ultimate source of absolute love.

*A loving thought
is a gift
that lasts for an eternity.*

The true teacher in life is direct experience. The following story is about one of my pupils who is a mother.

One day in meditation class, after observing this student, I sensed a beautiful change had occurred. I inquired about her previous week and she responded that the only memorable incident she could recall occurred one night when she was helping her daughter with her homework. As she leaned over her daughter's shoulder, their eyes met and their minds touched softly. In that fleeting instant a loving feeling was conveyed between their souls. This kind of love is exchanged only when we are being who we are. Pure and simple love in the silence of a moment flowed effortlessly from one to the other and back again in an extraordinary way. The far-reaching effects of love from this tender moment will bond this mother and daughter for all the days of their lives.

When a child is touched with the warm glow of love, the nature of her being is brightened. A precious gift is passed from parent to child that in turn will be passed to all those who cross these individuals' paths. When we walk in the light of love, life is a remarkable journey.

Love is the most precious gift we can share with each other. In the quiet of a moment feel a loving thought toward yourself and pass that gift to another. The present you give is a living gift that can touch another soul for an eternity.

*If someone cannot see
and appreciate your beauty within,
they are not worthy of it.*

If you are a sensitive person who is naturally open to love, one of your hardest lessons will be to learn not to permit others to walk all over you. Allowing another's dysfunction to become yours helps no one. Those who believe that enduring mistreatment will somehow make them a better person are self-abusive.

I had to learn this lesson the hard way. Before I met my wife, I had a couple of girlfriends who did not exactly display loving behavior toward me. On one occasion after an upsetting episode, I confided in a dear friend, who remarked, "Maybe you should lie flatter so she can walk on you easier." His words were a wake-up call. Shortly after we talked, I realized that if someone was incapable of seeing and appreciating my inner beauty, they were not worthy of being close to my heart.

Emotional pain is one of the greatest motivating forces on the planet, but it is valuable only if you learn from it. Without inner turmoil many people would do nothing to change their situation. Allow others close to your heart—your spiritual sanctuary—*only* if they love you enough to not hurt you. Protecting your heart in no way means blocking your expression of love: Real love is not about agony, it is about releasing yourself from it.

Without the courage to persevere and allow *genuine love* into your heart, what is the point of living?

The greatest joy in life is to give the gift of your love to someone who appreciates it. When your love is received as the priceless gift it is, the more you give away, the richer you become.

Loving without feeling
is like being a mannequin,
an inanimate expression of life.

Many people operate strictly on an intellectual level because this allows them to avoid the perils of heartache. When you experience love from your intellect, it becomes a representation of what you *think* love should be. True love cannot be intellectualized, it must be *felt* from your heart or it is not love. Real love is not manufactured; it is an expression from your heart and the basis of your true spiritual nature. Love without feeling is like being a mannequin; love without feeling is a lifeless expression.

It is sad to say, but many people feel unworthy of being loved. This is an inaccurate perception.

What is it that you feel you do not deserve?

What is it that you feel you do deserve?

Between these two questions is your heart's equilibrium. Find your unworthiness issues and you will understand the barriers to love. Release the barricades of resistance and love will simply manifest itself. Only when you persevere will you overcome your feelings of inferiority. No one is superior or inferior, everyone is just who they are. Learn to mentally massage your heart until you know every little detail about it. Feel your heart; love is centered at the core of your being.

One day, everyone will realize that love is our birthright to pursue and the pathway to complete freedom and happiness. Pure love is your true spiritual nature, who you are without masks or pretenses and the principal component of your entire being. Dissolve your mannequinlike identity and you will feel a warm, loving human being emerge.

*Any thought
within your soul
that is not love
is not the enlightened
nature of your being.*

Insecurities of the heart and inadequacies in the giving and receiving of love have many individual causes, but generally fall into two categories.

When emotional baggage from a role model is passed on to you as a negative trait, it becomes an affliction of the soul. Inferiority complexes inadvertently taken to heart are like viruses, passed from one person to another via dysfunction. Remember, any thought in your soul that is not love is not really the true you.

The second most common reason people have difficulties in the giving and receiving of love is because they have missing pieces of their soul relating to love. It is the fear of getting hurt which keeps everyone isolated from love. Without an awareness of the true nature of your being, you are blind to the knowledge within that only love can set your soul free. Love is realized by allowing your conscious awareness to be in a mindful tranquil space. Being detached from preconceived ideas, biases, and conditioning allows the mind to experience all of the variations required, to complete the picture of love.

The only hell on earth is the absence of love; it is not a fiery place but a state of mind in a person who is scared to look inside himself. Dissolve your painful compartmentalizations within and you are on the way to the realization of love.

The timeless answers to mankind's spiritual questions have been said by every master who has walked the earth, and yes, they have not changed. The answers you seek to love are within your own heart and can be understood through a patient mind.

Lessons in the giving and receiving of love
are doors to self-realization,
opening your heart and soul
to spiritual understanding.

There is so much struggle in the world and the solution is so simple. Do not negate the endowment that is already within you, your ability to love! The lessons of love appear in many variations, but are of two kinds: giving and receiving.

The giving of love seems to be easier for most people because they have some sense of control in the exchange. But along with the giving of love can come expectations, conditions, and control issues. The moment love is altered, it stops being love and becomes selfishness. Love associated with conditions easily becomes a mind game, creating separation, overshadowing the purity of love by competitive behavior. Is your love a game to win or lose or a tender interplay?

The receiving of love is much more difficult because it means acceptance, and requires vulnerability and trust. The most sacred trust is loving your own heart. If you cannot trust your own heart, you cannot trust another's. How can you love if you do not trust?

A common fear arises when you are learning to accept love. *If I drop my protective walls, I'll be hurt.* If you have walls interfering with love, are you not already miserable?

If you never bare your soul to love, you will never know the ecstasy of it. Surrender to love, let go of your fearful resistance, and love will embrace you. Relax your conscious awareness, open the portals of your heart, and allow love to fill your being. The portals of self-realization are within each individual; they are passageways to love. Do not fight your saving grace, yield your conscious awareness to love and it will draw you to the heavens.

Love
costs you nothing to give,
but costs you everything
when you cannot.

Many people have great difficulty giving love, as if it were a strenuous task. When you cannot give love, you will suffer. The coldness of a closed heart hurts most the person who possesses it, while indirectly creating a chilly atmosphere for all those around.

What will your soul give up by opening your heart to love?

Heartache and emotional pain lock the door to love. The obstructions people have around their hearts range from simple to elaborate. The most complicated protection devices are self-created security systems with layers of justifications for and rationalizations of why they either can't love or how they should love. Even simple defenses force you to protect your heart and be cautious in love.

If a defense mechanism of your own design keeps you from what you want to experience, who is shut out?

Your own stubborn refusal to open your heart permanently locks love out and leaves you in loneliness. Feel your heart with your conscious awareness. If you feel pain, contemplate its origin. It is an opportunity to open a door to realization. The master key to unlocking love's mysteries lies in understanding why you cannot open yourself to love.

Everyone has times when they are alone and their heart aches. In these times go within, and with great sensitivity, gently hold yourself. Feel kindness and love for yourself as if you are the most precious baby bird imaginable. When you can hold yourself in this way, your heart will take flight and the warm glow of love will begin to replace sorrow.

*The mind
is the navigator to the heavens,
with stillness
illumining the soul's reference points
to guide you.*

Seven

What Are the Reference Points within Your Mind?

Sense consciousness
is the eyes and the ears of our brain
but not the heart and soul
whence we derive our meaning.

Our five senses—sight, hearing, touch, taste, and smell—are the liaison between the physical world and our inner world. The primary form of consciousness people use is sense consciousness; it is part of our animalistic nature and is necessary for functioning in the outside world.

The brain receives information from sense consciousness, filing each new experience in our memories. If biases, cravings, or attachments cloud our perception, false observations are made. Clear interpretation of incoming information is vital for well-being.

Sense consciousness can make us feel good physically and mentally, but not necessarily at peace in our heart and soul. Relax your brain activity and sense consciousness perception will allow your conscious awareness to experience life through the spiritual sense of your soul. Walk with your conscious awareness in your heart and you will absorb all that the physical world has to offer. The merging of the physical senses with one's spiritual essence is like experiencing a beautiful dream only to find it is reality.

The reality of life is that we are all ultimately a reflection of our spiritual essence. If what you experience from within is not loving and kind, you have not found your true spiritual essence. Each time you do The QM Practice, you are loving yourself. Each time you love yourself, you are one step closer to your heart and the source of all that is meaningful.

*The brain runs the physical self,
but who operates the brain;
what do you know
about what motivates you?*

The brain is essentially an organic computer. It stores incoming information as memory and runs the daily operation of living based on self-preservation, but it does not inherently possess the wisdom that arises from one's essence, allowing one to know the difference between what is healthy and what is damaging.

The brain is the autopilot of our being and is magnificent when it is running correctly, allowing the conscious awareness to work uninterrupted in daily life. This autopilot tells us when to eat, when to sleep, and when the body needs attention. Problems occur when negative psychological patterns overrule our instinctual guide to health—for instance, overeating, excessive drinking, or any addictive compulsion to stimulate the senses. Only through the independent awareness of a conscious observing mind can we understand such patterns, detach ourselves from them, and become able to make clear choices.

For many people, the brain or small mind, has been giving orders for so long that they have forgotten who is in charge. For the most part, the brain makes decisions without an alert, objective conscious awareness. Allow your conscious awareness, in conjunction with your true nature, to run the business of living and let your brain do what it does best: direct the physical self.

Train your intellect to be quiet each day and you will begin to feel a fine relationship emerge between your brain, your conscious awareness, and the deep spiritual nature of your being.

*The battle for dominance
between the small mind and big mind
is a war that is ultimately won
by giving up the fight.*

The brain, or small mind, in its untrained state, is renegade energy that seems to have a will of its own; its repetitive, chattering thoughts operate without rhyme or reason. Its overriding goal is to find pleasure and avoid pain. The small mind holds on to the past, maintaining a familiar standard in the name of security, even if it is detrimental. Gratification of the senses is sought at any cost. When physical pleasure is used to avoid pain, dysfunction results—excessive eating, drinking, use of drugs, etc.

The small mind is simply a memory facility and operations manager for the physical body. The untrained small mind does not know what is needed for spiritual well-being. It does not know that by facing your pain you dissolve it. It does not know that excessive physical gratification can be harmful. It operates on the pleasure principle and is thus usually in opposition to your spiritual self—or big mind—which knows what your true being really needs.

Allowing your conscious awareness to become still at a single point within diverts energy from the brain's resistant patterns. The battle within finally ends when your brain realizes that without guidance from your big mind, life lacks meaning.

The battle for dominance between your small mind and big mind *consciously* begins when you start The QM Practice. Ending the conflict within is achieved by designating time for your personal spiritual development so you can recognize uncontrolled thoughts, dismantle them, and allow your mind to work in harmony. The QM Practice will teach you.

*The small mind and big mind
are like two different people
with dissimilar perspectives.
What dominates your life:
patterns from your brain
or the true nature of your being?*

When you talk to yourself, who is the other person and what do they say? Fluent communication between your small mind and big mind depends on how effortlessly the two relate with each other. If you fight and get angry at yourself, your small mind and big mind are merely rivals.

Do you enjoy your relationship with yourself?

The small mind is strongly repetitive; once the motion of thought begins, it has difficulty stopping. It operates within established routines and does not like change, often resisting the assimilation of new information.

People use their intellects more than their hearts because our culture emphasizes the thinking process over feelings. Importance is placed on the Intelligence Quotient while the Emotional Quotient is ignored. In society, the relevance of what we feel is secondary, but in actuality, our feelings govern the quality of our life and whether we want to live or die. In a healthy small mind/big mind relationship, there is a harmonious interplay between the thinking and feeling processes.

Look at your meditation practice as if it were a marriage, an opportunity to balance the relationship between what you think and how you feel. Nurture your meditation, and your conscious awareness will give your brain the needed space to unravel its complexities. Everyone needs inner space. The QM Practice provides a way to experience the timeless bounds of mind.

*Conscious awareness
within individuals
ranges between those who are oblivious
to those who are mindful.*

Conscious awareness is the part of you that observes what you are thinking about. When conscious awareness is untrained, clear observations and perceptions are weak, and you have a tendency to be controlled by the past.

When conscious awareness is used properly, it illuminates the undefined parts of your mind. In other words, when conscious awareness is associated with your big mind—your spiritual self—you are liberated, gaining the ability to move freely within the overall framework of the mind. This freedom gives you the opportunity to make decisions without resistance from the small mind's old patterns of thinking. Independent conscious awareness gives you the option to choose which part of your mind to function from; the past conditioning of the small mind or the immediate experience of the big mind.

Do you want to live a life based on patterns from your brain, or from the perceptions of your big mind—perceptions free of influences from the past?

Conscious awareness is the first major reference point to notice when practicing Quiescence Meditation. It is important to be able to calm your conscious awareness on command and to relax the brain. Learning to relax the conscious awareness and to detach yourself from the clamoring of the small mind are two very important mental disciplines to master. Relaxing your conscious awareness through the brain network is highly therapeutic for relieving mental stress and allows you to drop into deeper states of meditation.

When conscious awareness is detached from brain function, mindfulness and enlightenment are sure to follow.

*Independent conscious awareness
brings you to the realization
that freedom is won
when you are no longer ruled by fear.*

As we proceed through life, events we participate in and observe help form the foundation of who we are. When occurrences are pleasing, it is common to re-create experiences because we fear a new one won't meet our expectations. Problems begin when we cling to memories and try to duplicate an original emotion. It appears to work the first few times, but eventually becomes a trap and limits our ability to experience life as it is.

If your brain rules your conscious awareness, you cannot be free in the moment. When your brain will not release your conscious awareness, you will be bound to your past, leaving you tied to what was rather than open to new experiences in every moment.

The QM Practice teaches you how to utilize your conscious awareness and disengage from analytical brain function. As this change begins to occur, one of the most prevalent fears—fear of change—wells up. As you begin releasing your old conditioned self, another fear arises. *Who will I be if I let go of my patterned personality?* The answer is simple. *You will be who you are without fear, able to experience each moment with more freedom.*

When your conscious awareness is allied with your true nature, you will perceive reality clearly. A free conscious awareness does not cling to the past; it knows only how to live in the present without fear. Direct your conscious awareness within and you will find where the real experience of life is realized and lived.

*Ðetaching conscious awareness
from the small mind slave driver
requires practice, persistence, and patience.*

When brain function operates independent of your big mind, it tends to waste time and energy, being driven by fear and insecurity. The patterns from your brain are like a slave driver, relentlessly prodding, even when this is done at your own expense. Freeing your conscious awareness from this taskmaster takes practice, persistence, and patience.

But when your awareness detaches and awakens, your capacity to experience life flourishes. You begin to perceive and think from a clear independent perspective, free of your old programming. Your conscious awareness begins to instruct your slave-driving brain instead of the other way around. You become mindful of your actions; your ability to comprehend comes with greater ease and enjoyment because you no longer operate from obsolete "tapes." You can stay in the moment because you do not want to leave it; all you care to be in is the now. You begin to feel alive as you never felt before, and a new world opens before your eyes.

With practice, persistence, and patience, you will begin to understand the independent function of your conscious awareness. You will shift from operating in brain function to mind function. Transformation of your conscious awareness is one of the silent miracles that happens as a result of The QM Practice. Many people talk about what it would be like to have an untroubled mind. Here is a way to experience freedom firsthand—by detaching your conscious awareness from the small mind slave driver, you literally set your spirit free.

*The surface of the mind
is a horizontal plane
of electrochemical energy
that exists between the outside world
of sense consciousness
and the inside world
of subtlety and spirituality.*

If you close your eyes and feel where you understand these words, you will notice where your thinking process is located: it is a subtle horizontal plane of electrochemical energy directly at eye level. This is where your intellectual knowledge of the linear-based outside world meets your spiritual nonlinear inside world.

The intellect—the brain—in conjunction with the surface of the mind, understands the outside world by dissecting incoming data. The intellect evaluates information in linear time by sequentially measuring the movement of matter through space.

All thought below the surface of the mind is relative to the spiritual, inner world. It is a world without solid form or linear time and correlates with matters of the heart and feelings. A full and complete life is a harmonious relationship between how you think about the outside world and how you feel about yourself, with the ability to move freely between the two.

The surface of the mind helps you to have a panoramic view. Consciously *feeling* and being able to identify the surface of the mind is paramount when you begin The QM Practice. When you find this reference point, you can begin to calm the surface of your mind with confidence and knowing. Only when you understand how your mind works can you effectively use it.

The predicament human beings face, lies in their not caring to understand what drives them, a decision to walk in ignorance. Ignorance perpetuates suffering and is a black mark on mankind's history.

How many black marks must you endure before you learn?

*Carrying the weight of the world
on the surface of your mind
only encumbers your walk through life.*

When too many thoughts move across the surface of your mind, they create ripples. As more thoughts cross your mind, the surface becomes choppy; add still more thoughts and you have waves, leading to a storm of thought. Mental storms twist incoming information into an indistinguishable reality. It is quite common for people to perpetually carry unfinished business on their minds; this produces hurry and a frantic scramble to catch up. The situation worsens when unattended matters accumulate on the surface of the mind and are forgotten over time, becoming permanent dysfunction. It is not unusual to have layers of behavioral patterns on the surface of the mind, interacting with each other to form closed loops of delusion.

Counterproductive ways of being detract from living harmoniously in the here and now. Accepting or putting up with oppression on the surface of the mind is a self-induced labor camp, with you deciding the length of your sentence.

The surface of the mind is a receptor, not a collector. Anything that is allowed to collect on the surface of your mind will hinder reception of incoming data. Dysfunctional programs at the surface of the mind limit your ability to think and perceive clearly. Unless the surface of the mind is cleansed on a regular basis with stillness, negative programs will not be released; your conscious awareness will continue to be confused and uncertain as you plod through life.

Your walk through life is a perception from your own mind; only when you know your mind will you lessen the burdens that weigh you down.

*Mental consciousness
is the link
between the outside physical world
and the inside world of images.*

Mental consciousness is an intellectual process we use when our physical senses are not in operation. It is the thinking process. Mental consciousness is most often utilized when we read, add and subtract numbers, or when we visualize in our head. Mental consciousness is located at the center of the surface of the mind and is associated with brain function. It is more closely affiliated with thinking than with the feeling nature of our being; it is the reference point where the brain operates without distraction from the five physical senses.

This reference point, at the surface of the mind provides a place of convergence where conscious awareness can operate without diversions from the outside world. When one uses mental consciousness, the outside world fades away simply because you are not preoccupied with it; this is natural concentration.

Mental consciousness is a work area. It allows your conscious awareness to process information unencumbered by outside influences. This is not necessarily where we determine if something is good or bad, right or wrong. Conscience only comes into play by connecting with your spiritual nature, which is found through exploring your heart and soul.

*The surface of the mind
is the superficial edge
of an immense spiritual oasis within.*

Each time you still the surface of the mind, it becomes like a two-sided mirror reflecting everything outside you and within you. The top side of the mirror pertains to the thinking process, while the bottom side relates to how you feel about yourself.

Emotional problems originate as negative experiences registered at the surface of the mind. If an experience is traumatic and you take it to heart, it sinks within your soul and becomes negative debris trapped within you. Mental garbage is anything that separates your conscious awareness from your true nature. Signals are sent to the surface of your mind from within when you respond with emotion to a situation in the outside world. If feelings sent to the surface are harmonious and nonresistant, no problems occur. But when negative, resistant energy ripples the surface of your mind from below, disharmonious feelings create difficulties you cannot run away from.

People avoid emotional pain because they do not know what to do when it surfaces. Facing emotional debris takes less energy than you might think. In fact, when you learn to detach from psychological baggage without ignoring it, you will dissipate it. Dissolving discontentment that prevents you from opening your heart is a miracle you can experience.

Every time you sit down and practice this form of meditation it is like activating an internal waterfall, washing out psychological debris from your spiritual oasis. The QM Practice helps you reclaim an oasis that is rightfully yours, a genuine wonder of the universe and necessary for spiritual well-being.

If the source of your spiritual replenishment is polluted, what will sustain you when you are thirsty?

Everyone
is yearning to uncover
the wondrous field of energy within
that is the entrance
to your heart and soul.

We all have experienced emotions that well up from within and bring tears to our eyes. These feelings come from a field of energy below the surface of the mind. It appears like a cone of unending, iridescent, shimmering energy. It is the limitless space within yourself that contains the origins of your true spiritual nature. All on the planet who are seeking spiritual fulfillment are looking for this space; it is known in ancient Sanskrit as *kelee* (pronounced "key-lee") which means "having to do with different states of mind."

Each time you release emotional blocks from the kelee cone, indescribable feelings of well-being emerge; known as *sumadhi* in Sanskrit, it is a state of extraordinary bliss, and can only be truly comprehended by personal experience. Living from this space becomes a wondrous, magical adventure, much like how a loving child sees the world.

When everyone learns how to direct their conscious awareness to a still point within their kelee cone of energy, resistance on the planet will drop dramatically. Fear will dissipate and the ability to love without pain will come to pass. Silent miracles will happen everywhere and to everyone. Spirituality will be defined by one's loving and compassionate actions, instead of mere professions of spirituality while actions continue to express something quite different. Love will replace fear and humankind will realize that the way is within and has always been so.

The refuge everyone seeks
is not a place,
but a state of mind.
Yield to your true spiritual nature
and you will become your sanctuary.

Eight

What Can The Quiescence Meditation Practice Do for You?

The Quiescence Meditation Practice
is not a belief system;
it is a way
to simply unravel the mind's complexity.

The concept of stillness in the mind is so simple, it actually baffles the intellect. The QM way of stilling your mind is unique in its approach. The QM Practice is not a belief system. Belief systems are secondhand knowledge. You may believe something to be so, but you never truly know unless you have firsthand experience. For example, I can believe I know what Mexican food tastes like after reading a cookbook, but without the real experience of tasting the food, my knowledge is secondhand. When you do The QM Practice, your experience is firsthand; you will savor the real enchilada.

The QM Practice is applicable regardless of your religious or philosophical background. It is irrelevant what your occupation is; an orderly mind will clearly and positively improve your life. You do not have to commit to a cause, become a devotee, do weird rituals, or sit for hours at a time. The Practice requires short periods of quality time in stillness as a part of your daily routine.

From a still mind, *receptive conscious awareness* evolves into the means to understanding your heart, mind, and soul. The stillness allows your awareness to access your true nature, which in turn organizes the mind perfectly. As with all endeavors of value, practice is everything. Allow your mind to quiet naturally, and belief systems will be replaced by direct experience as your true nature is realized over time.

The QM Practice
illumines
the quandaries of the mind
into states of understanding.

To understand The QM Practice let's start with a simple concept: stillness of thought. Anything that is not still is in motion. When you are thinking, the energy from your thoughts generates movement in your mind. The energy from thought movement is doing *something*, but the question is what?

Does the movement from your thoughts meet with your approval?

If not, how can you bring about a change?

To truly experience and understand anything your mind must be free of preconceived thoughts or be in a state known as *beginner's mind*. Beginner's mind is a state of freedom from previously formed opinions. In this state, the surface of the mind resembles a clean blackboard; there is a clear space to write on and learn from. For example, when you put one math problem on a clean blackboard, you are able to concentrate with ease. If you fill up the blackboard and write on top of existing equations, your ability to concentrate becomes fragmented, making it difficult to compute without distraction. When your conscious awareness is contending with more than one thought, your mind becomes scattered. If your thinking drifts onto something other than what you are doing, you are wandering. However, if you focus on one thought at a time, you are concentrating.

If your mind is not focused on what you are doing, it is somewhere else! Be where you are and you will experience what you are doing. The QM Practice is a means to bring you into the moment, this one, right now!

*Silence can be defined
in two diametrically opposed ways:
as a burying of painful memories
by being closemouthed and bottled up,
or as a quiet peaceful mind,
free of distressing thoughts,
open to the freedom of self-expression.*

When people bury painful memories and feelings, they become like a volcano of emotion waiting to erupt. The type of outburst will vary, depending on the severity of the emotion and how long it has been stuffed. Everyone knows someone who, when upset, becomes silent. Just because an individual is not talking does not mean they have nothing to say. Suppressed animosity usually means the individual has a lot to say but does not know how to express it. When someone gives you the silent treatment, it is as if they are waving a red flag saying, "I need help but do not know how to ask for it." When you observe contained hostility in a friend or loved one, be kind and gentle; your calmness will help defuse their wrath.

The most powerful and healthy form of silence is produced by a quiet mind. There are no obstacles too large for a still mind to overcome. This form of silence is achieved in meditation, when you allow your thought activity to slow to the purest state of complete stillness. Upon completing your practice, immediately after stillness, your mind can experience perfect receptivity. When your conscious awareness is calm and receptive, you will expand mindfulness. Ultimately, everyone is looking to master mindfulness, because the answers to life's questions are found there.

The QM Practice is like building a bridge, helping you get from where you are to where you want to be. Silence in meditation serves to clear a pathway to understanding; it illuminates the structures within your mind that no longer serve you, and dissolves them. It is easy to do; you have nothing to lose but painful memories and fears that block your way to mindfulness.

Stillness
is like a tuning fork for the mind:
it attunes you
to the harmony
or discord of your own vibration.

In The QM Practice, stillness is crucial; it is like a tuning fork for your mind. Everyone has heard the expression "being in tune." Well, being in tune takes on a new meaning when you understand that we are composed of energy and each one of us has a slightly different vibration. We are all like bells of varying shapes and sizes, with each person producing a unique resonance. Your thoughts cast the mold for the shape, size, and vibratory rate of your soul's resonance.

If your vibration is sharp, you have too much ego; your pitch is too high and needs softening. Sharp vibrations, emitting a cutting or piercing tone, are offensive to others, much like someone who is boisterous and brags about what they have or what they do. Quiescence Meditation will moderate the sharpness of this person's energy and smooth it to a harmonious tone.

If your vibration is flat, you lack self-confidence. Flat vibrations are dull, lifeless, and somber. The uncertainty produced from a flat vibration projects apprehension and lends itself to mediocrity. The QM Practice will help raise this person's vibration by deleting negative patterns, which send out chords that are too low and bothersome to others.

Stillness enables us to determine if our vibration is off-key. When each person learns to tune their own mind, the unique intonation from each individual vibration will join in the universal symphony of life, with everyone a virtuoso playing at perfect pitch. Your mind is an incredible instrument. Is it in tune?

*The QM Practice
calls for a lifetime dedication
to studying your mind,
with mindfulness as the goal
and happiness as your reward.*

The first few months of practicing Quiescence Meditation are the most crucial, because during this time it is so easy to give up. Until you see the fruits of your labor, you will probably feel perplexed and wonder if you are doing The Practice correctly or question if The Practice works at all. Stilling your mind is extremely hard to do.

Do not give up before the miracle happens!

Being at a complete still point in your kelee cone will take much practice and patience. The rewards from The Practice come in your everyday life, not while you are in meditation. Initially, watch for a general calming of your overall vibration. Depending on the individual, this can be startlingly obvious or extremely subtle. As you continue to practice, a transformation begins happening. Changes can take place as early as the first few weeks, while others will come with time. It is an ongoing process. The short-term goal of practicing Quiescence Meditation is to put an end to your discontent and free yourself from suffering. The long-term goal is to become absolute love.

As one day moves into the next and you look back at the time invested in your practice, you will notice how your values have changed. You will find yourself being drawn to endeavors that concern your well-being and inner peace. Seemingly insignificant activities and observations bring joy for no particular apparent reason. It will seem as if a breath of fresh air has wafted into your life. This will be you, free of your own constraints, on the pathway to mindfulness and lasting happiness.

*Mindfulness cultivates
the ability to concentrate completely
on a single thing
and the capacity to expand perception
to infinity.*

The ability to focus on one thing at a time is vitally important for mindfulness and a sense of well-being. When you learn to concentrate on a single thing, an interesting phenomenon begins to happen: instead of having your conscious awareness spread over five different tasks at once, you become aware of and work on five distinct elements within a given task. This form of concentration happens when you become so absorbed in what you are doing that you do not notice distracting sounds and outside movements. Even the most mundane job can bring a sense of fulfillment, when your mind is earnestly focused.

Several years ago a Tibetan Buddhist master gave me the title of Master of the Mundane in front of a large group of people. Everyone in the audience laughed. At the time I was embarrassed, not recognizing that this teacher does not call anyone a master of anything readily or lightly. He gave me the title because I have the ability to immerse myself in the most mundane of tasks and enjoy what I do in a pure and natural state of being.

At the opposite end of the spectrum is the ability to open your awareness to the immeasurable, which is necessary to understand the big picture of life. A wide expanse of awareness allows you to stand back and evaluate a situation from a broader perspective, preventing the mind from becoming narrow and stuck in rigid ways of being.

The QM Practice trains your mind to be in one place at a time with the ability to change focus on command.

*The human "race" is not a sprint
to acquire the knowledge of life,
but a comprehension of
how to stand still and enjoy it.*

As your mind relaxes, you begin to recognize that the way to happiness is not through aggression but in finding your true spiritual nature. As we move from the animalistic side of our nature to a more spiritual one, adrenaline for fight-or-flight is needed less and less. Running for our life or fighting to get out of dangerous situations calls on our instinct for self-preservation, but as the higher functions of our spiritual mind awaken, we steer ourselves away from predicaments where we have to fear for our lives.

By eliminating blockages that obscure your true nature, you begin experiencing conscious self-control in a new way; you are no longer ruled by fear! Your newly developing awareness heightens how you think and feel. Simple daily activities such as combing your hair become enjoyable instead of a chore. Brushing your teeth becomes a massage for your mouth. The beautiful changes are endless as you find yourself growing into a person you would like to be.

The Practice will initiate physical changes; you will become calm as your body begins releasing endorphins and natural tranquilizers. The body's immune system and ability to heal itself becomes activated, promoting health and well-being. You simply begin to enjoy your life.

In the meantime you find yourself becoming more spiritual by being the person you really are. Your presence affects people in a comforting way that brings smiles and uplifts spirits.

Liberate your soul from the confines of fear, worry, and discontent and you will live an extraordinary life.

*The Quiescence Meditation Practice
is a pathway to self-understanding,
not a competition to reach a destination.*

Open your mind to The QM Practice; it is a restorative exercise of the highest quality. The Practice is calming, thought provoking, and mentally challenging. It also offers the highest degree of personal spiritual attainment and gives the practitioner a remarkable sense of fulfillment.

Patience is extremely important. Go slow!

Ponder this: If someone is leisurely walking down a road from point A to point B and another person is driving down the same road at sixty-five miles an hour, who will have seen more of their surroundings when they arrive at point B?

This practice offers individual understanding on the road of life. Do not worry about how long it takes to arrive at your destination. The purpose of life is to travel well. When you are patient enough just to be, the pace of your journey will decelerate, allowing a newly developing awareness of the deeper meaning of life.

The rewards from doing The Practice will dawn on you when you least expect it, startling you as you realize how little of life you have actually been experiencing. You will begin to understand more. You will become aware of the problems in the world, but will be unaffected by them because inner contentment sustains you. You will recognize that people are suffering, with no idea of how to free themselves. As your true nature grows, you will begin to teach and inspire with your calm radiant presence.

The longer you do The Practice the more beautiful your being becomes. It will seem like a miracle, although you will have no way to explain it because it is silent. When you love how you live, you have arrived at the meaning of life.

The true nature of your spiritual essence,
cannot be experienced
until your conscious awareness
is free enough to feel without fear.

You cannot access your true spiritual nature until you have dealt with the resistance that blocks your path inward. Fear, anger, and worry are the matters that will be addressed first when you begin The Practice. As these points of resistance dissolve, it is common for many beginners to become apprehensive and feel vulnerable without their walls to protect them. It may seem like you are reverting back to old patterns, but this is not so; your anxiety is a signal that you are breaking through and destroying the blockages. Be kind and patient with yourself when you are releasing resistance or you will add unnecessary frustration. Also, bear in mind that as each electrochemical point of resistance dissolves, it will be the last time you will experience the emotional uneasiness from that particular dysfunction.

As you begin letting go of your unwanted patterns, periods of happiness and contentment begin to emerge in place of counterproductive ways of being. As longer periods of harmony become your standard, you have less tolerance for needless mental discomfort. At the same time your sensitivity to mental pain becomes an early-warning system, allowing you to become aware of distress before it becomes an issue.

Do not measure your progress too harshly; processing fear and resistance calls for patience. Never forget what a beautiful gift you are giving to yourself every time you sit down and practice meditation, even if the quality of the stillness may not be as good as you would like. As long as you keep trying, the results will come.

*What most people commonly call moods
are known in
The Quiescence Meditation Practice
as processing or dissolving dysfunction.*

For most people, life is experienced as a succession of moods, many of them seemingly inflicted upon them, for some unknown reason. After beginning The QM Practice, you'll be able to objectively observe dysfunction and understand the reasons for your moods. As your conscious awareness begins to drop its protective walls, you temporarily uncover points of resistance within you. Dropping your walls can sometimes feel uncomfortable, until the resistance completely dissolves. So, what most people commonly call moods, in The QM Practice, changes into the processing of dysfunction.

Occasionally, QM students come to class and express that they have been upset or grouchy for the past few days, forgetting that what The Practice does is reveal dysfunction. I constantly remind students to look at processing as a sign that The Practice is working; you are growing while letting go of dysfunction. Remember, do not inflict your discomfort on others while processing; let your family or friends know you need to be by yourself until the distress passes. Physical exercise, especially in nature, helps immensely when processing.

Just remember, as the negative state of mind passes, it will be the last time you will experience the emotion from that particular button. Also bear in mind that when processing, you may not feel like doing your practice, but this is when you need to do it most. Do your practice regardless of the discomfort. If you do not, you will only drag out the release of the problem.

Wise men
have known for centuries
the wisdom gleaned
from a mind that is still.

There is a story about a wise old man who quietly awakens and ponders the significance of his life. As the morning light brightens, he looks up at the sky while a bird flies by and he observes the quiet sound of the wind rustling through the bird's wings. Throughout his daily activities, his mind is content with the fluid passage of time. At the end of the day, the old man feels a profound connection between himself and his world. As he slowly makes his way to bed, the sun dips behind the clouds; beautiful images of the day drift by and happiness warms his soul.

How many people really take the time to experience, from the depths of their being, the world around them?

Stillness within will open your eyes to a new world, producing an awareness beyond physical bounds, transcending all time and space. Over time a still, aware mind has the power to illumine a soul to full enlightenment.

If stilling the mind is such a powerful tool for personal change, why do not more people meditate? Because one cannot miss what one has never known!

How does stillness of mind illuminate wisdom? A still, receptive mind simply gives you the opportunity to observe clearly. From an unobstructed vantage point, your conscious awareness is able to function unimpeded, free from internal and external distractions, able to truly absorb the lessons the world has to offer.

Sages and wise men are called such for a reason: they know a still, receptive mind commands clarity and the ability to understand the nature of the universe itself.

*The QM Practice in its purest form
is stillness of the mind—
clearing the mind to contemplate
life's most important questions.*

What can Quiescence Meditation do for you? Nothing and everything at the same time. The Practice teaches nothing about controlling others and everything about how to control yourself.

If you do not deliberately take the time to quiet your mind, when will it happen? By accident, happenstance, or when circumstances in the outside world cooperate? How often does that occur? And what about the influences from your inside world? How do you get away from the chatter within your own mind?

The Quiescence Meditation method calls for practice, diligence, and patience. A still mind broadens consciousness and brings clarity to any situation, providing a point of reference from which all things can be seen as they truly are. The QM Practice is a pathway to find the answers to the three most important questions you can ask yourself:

1. Who are you and how do you find your true spiritual nature?

2. Why are you here and how do you release yourself from that which keeps you bound to pain and suffering?

3. Where are you going and does your pathway lead to absolute love?

When you are patient, you will find who you are.

When you are in the moment, you will find why you are here.

When your mind is calm, you will see where you are going.

*The awe-inspiring space
of your true spiritual nature
is tranquillity
beyond intellectualization.*

Nine

How Finding Your True Nature Leads to Enlightenment

*Everyone is on a pathway
to find their true spiritual nature,
whether
they are aware of it or not.*

We are all looking for self-acceptance, but if we look for it in anything other than ourselves, we will never find it. We can spend countless hours trying to be who we are told we should be, but if we are unaware of our true nature, we will never be who we really are!

When your conscious awareness becomes one with your true nature, you will no longer feel the need to prove yourself. When awareness of your thoughts is clear, they actualize, allowing your destiny to emerge from within.

As you begin practicing Quiescence Meditation, you begin to understand why you have difficulty being who you really are. Slowly, the light from within brightens, until the feeling of internal poverty dissipates, allowing your true spiritual nature to inspire you. You will begin to sense an order in the universe and a feeling that everything is as it should be.

Your true nature is the essence of all life; it is a ceaseless river within you. Having the courage to jump into the river means taking responsibility for your internal dysfunction. It also means enjoying the endless beauty and love that results from being brave enough to face what many turn away from.

If you turn away from the true spiritual nature of your being, in what direction are you heading?

*Respect for nature
is an exquisite reflection
of a person who has learned to appreciate
the nature of his inner world.*

Have you ever witnessed someone litter? What does that behavior say about a person?

Littering is a reflection of a spiritual wasteland within a disorderly soul. What emanates from an impoverished soul ends up as garbage in the world. Now someone has to clean up what another has done out of wanton disregard. Upon cultivating an appreciation of your true spiritual nature, you simply will not act irresponsibly, you will respect your surroundings.

Man is the only creature on the planet who can trash not only his environment but himself, with impure thoughts manifesting themselves in the outside world as reality. When an individual's mind is polluted with selfish, self-destructive, unenlightened thoughts, everyone suffers. Illumination through education and awareness is the way to inspire change within and prevent environmental degradation.

The QM Practice raises self-awareness and will teach you how to change the environment of your mind through the cleansing practice of stillness. And when everyone takes responsibility for their own actions through mindful awareness, the ground will be cleaner, our water will be purer, and our skies will be clearer. We will be able to appreciate and love all of nature. Collectively, everyone will be on a wonderful pathway to being one with themselves and one with nature.

*All of the desecration in the world
is a direct result
of what people
have done out of ignorance.*

There are two types of catastrophes in the world: acts of nature and man-made disasters. When it comes to natural occurrences, there is only so much we can do. But as far as man-made damage goes, there is a lot we can do. Consider this: If Homo sapiens were not here, there would be no disharmony on the planet. What does this say about civilized man?

When individuals work out the issues within themselves, we will collectively lessen the disorder in the world.

As you do The QM Practice, your connection with your true nature awakens you to your surroundings, both animate and inanimate. Care of the environment becomes a reflection of the way you take care of yourself. The spiritual essence of your being gives you a lucid awareness, so that you act with the insight of forethought rather than the stupidity of thoughtlessness. You learn to think clearly and intuitively know the right decisions to make. Your true nature will guide you. It has a remarkable way of discerning what is for the good of all.

When people learn to cleanse their minds, collectively we will clean up the world's problems. Ignorance is internal pestilence, manifesting itself as external affliction, and will be cured only by the light of awareness that emanates from a quiet mind. The answer is in everyone's hands right now. The responsibility to end mindless devastation is up to each one of us.

Awaken your intellectual process
with the true nature of your being;
open your sleepy eyes
and rise from the laziness
of a lethargic mind.

If the thinking process of the intellect is to help you achieve spiritual harmony, it must awaken to your true nature. It must transfer power to the part of your nature that knows what will set your soul free. The intellect, under the guidance of your true nature, will never compromise your welfare; it will unequivocally know what is for your utmost well-being.

The thinking process can run wild without the calm disposition from your true nature, but without the intellect, we would not be able to verbalize our feelings—expressing what causes suffering and what yields love. A common language must develop between what the intellect thinks and what our heart feels if our soul is to grow and know happiness. The experience of love will not unfold unless there is a connection between your heart and your intellect with an independent conscious awareness.

As you begin The QM Practice, you will realize that the spiritual eyes of your soul have been quite lazy. It is easy to see what needs to be done and find the energy to work on tasks in the outside world, but when it comes to your own internal spiritual development, you can be blind to your mission and your mind can be too lethargic. The QM Practice will help you wake yourself up; it will open your eyes and rouse your mind.

When an alert thinking process expresses what is felt in your heart, your spiritual eyes will glisten with the inner glow of awareness.

*Open your intellectual process
to the true spiritual nature of your being
and your conscious awareness
will realize wisdom.*

The intellect operates well in the physical world but struggles with the inner world of emotion and self-understanding. The intellect works well with facts, figures, and storing information, but when it comes to knowing right from wrong, it flounders.

Our society teaches us a great deal about using our brain, but what about our spiritual nature and the pursuit of deeper wisdom?

Our true nature works within the mode of direct experience while our brain network functions best within the manner of understood experience and prescribed limits. You may notice that most people are more comfortable following an established procedure someone else has already created; it is a rare person who has a strong intellect and can live spontaneously, free of their conditioning. From The QM Practice you will learn to listen to your true nature and follow nothing other than your own spiritual pathway.

The fundamental difference between your intellect and your true nature is that your intellect takes apart an experience to understand it, while your true nature perceives everything as a whole. A beautiful sunrise is a good example: the intellect will dissect the sunrise to understand all its components and why it is beautiful, while your true nature will simply enjoy what it is. Both experiences have merit, but many only opt for the intellectual approach alone.

Would it not be wise to use both ways?

Allow your conscious awareness to experience your true nature and self-understanding will become spiritual wisdom.

*The true nature of your being
is not a result of analysis;
it is knowing
through uninterrupted experience.*

An interesting thing transpires as you do The Practice. You begin to realize the difference between your intellect and the true nature of your mind. You become aware of the limitations of rationalizing, self-justification, or any thought pattern that drives you to impose your position on others.

Compulsive, insecure thought patterns often originate from a time when you were unsure of yourself. These mental programs of uncertainty can be many layers deep and leave us confused about the right course of action in any given situation. Layers of indecision can also fragment the mind's ability to focus, resulting in mental conditions like attention deficit disorder. Scattered conscious awareness has difficulty deciding where it should go, so it bounces between layers of energy, making it difficult for us to remain on one task. Stilling the mind at the surface dissolves the layers, thus ending the problem.

Your true nature, in association with your conscious awareness as an independent observer, works differently: it consults with the intellect, reviews information, and decides on a course of action from a heart level. Your heart knows right from wrong.

This is your next lesson: Trust your heart. When you find yourself unable to resolve a moral issue, and turn it over and over, seeing it from every angle but to no avail, quiet your mind, try to feel deep within for your answer. If resolution does not come, be patient. Doing nothing is far more powerful than doing something regrettable!

*Changing an experience before it forms
is like prying open a flower
before it blooms;
you alter its natural unfolding.*

The experience of understanding your true nature must be allowed to unfold in its own way or your intellect will interfere with it. After starting The Practice, many people begin to have deep spiritual realizations, but before these reveal themselves fully, the students get excited and interfere with the experience. Allow comprehension to completely form before you start to analyze. The revelations you seek can be destroyed by your own thoughts. Premature analysis is like prying open a rosebud before its time; you will only tear the flower apart.

The intellect is an important part of the mind, but taking orders is not one of its strong qualities. Brain function enjoys control; it also prefers to analyze how we feel instead of accepting what is. If our hearts are to open and blossom, we must trust in our hearts. Without confidence in our heart, love cannot be felt and we will block out love for fear of getting hurt.

The intellect tends to justify emotions while your true nature knows only how to experience what is felt. If you have not realized it by now, how you feel about your life means everything. If your heart is not in what you do, you are in a desolate place! Trust in your heart and it will expand and bloom into love. Allow the subtle guidance of your true nature to nurture your intellect.

When everyone is patient enough to permit life to unfold like a beautiful flower, humankind will realize that the Garden of Eden is a state of mind, ultimately creating a beautiful physical world.

*Our true spiritual nature
can only be realized
through direct experience;
anything else is speculation.*

You are the only person who can go within and experience your true spiritual nature. It is then that wondering becomes knowing. To understand your being, your mind must learn to cultivate sensitivity, receptivity, and awareness. Without the ability to perceive clearly for yourself, you can only theorize. Direct experience is the only way to know your true nature.

If you met Jesus or Buddha walking on a road and had the occasion to sit down and ask them questions, you would be fascinated and in awe of their presence, but how would you understand the deeper realms of their minds if you could not truly perceive them? All you could possibly do would be to try to grasp their insights through analysis. Even they, with all of their knowledge and wisdom, could not present you with Heaven or Nirvana. But in understanding the spiritual nature of your being, you can find these in yourself.

A true spiritual teacher inspires others to greatness by instructing students to still their mind, study their thoughts, and contemplate their actions. Your true nature is *yours* to find, not mine or anyone else's.

You have been introduced to a purification practice for the mind that works miracles. The QM Practice is not speculation, it simply works and all you have to do is do it.

*Effortless effort
is a way of being
that requires an awareness of subtle energy,
taking practice and patience to master.*

In teaching, I run across a multitude of mental programs that have been passed from parents to their children. An old-school work ethic seems to be that everything has to be earned by the sweat of your brow or it is not worthwhile having. Life does not have to be lived this way . . . unless you like to perspire. Mental exhaustion is a sure sign you are using more energy on a task than is necessary. The true nature of your being utilizes mindful awareness to accomplish a task. Work is still required, but it is a different kind of work; it is effortless effort resulting from a quiet, receptive, open mind.

There is an old saying: *hard work is good for the soul*. This statement is true, but not when negatively driven small-mind patterns have more power than the free will of your independent conscious awareness. The roots of this saying come from an era when most work was done outdoors, in association with nature. When one works in nature, a spaciousness in the mind opens and forms a soothing connection with your soul, evoking a feeling of being part of a greater whole. A sense of accomplishment is passed from your heart through your hands to an end product, and this brings enjoyment.

If you return in your mind to a time when you were happy in your work, you will notice that the work may have been strenuous but there was an ease in your mental state; this ease comes from a mind that is open. At the end of a long day your body may be physically tired but your mind is content.

The satisfaction everyone desires is mental peace and freedom, and using effortless energy is the way to master it.

*Subtle awareness
is like a soft breeze
emerging from our mind,
often bestowed upon one
who does not realize its significance.*

What all beings are ultimately seeking is not the cold finalities of analytical thought but the meaning of their true spiritual essence. Your essence is by nature subtle, timeless, ever-changing, and yet the same. The true nature of your being is as vast as the boundless universe and cannot be measured, only experienced with an acutely receptive conscious awareness.

As you begin to explore the space within that leads to your heart, your conscious' awareness will sense gentle, exquisite feelings that seem almost too good to be true. Introspection brings forth profound insights, but because subtle thoughts are so serene, they are easily drowned out by the brain's need to analyze. Subtle thought is poetry from the soul. As soothing as a lullaby, its lyrical message nudges the mind to a deeper understanding of life.

Relax into your essence. Simply be and you will begin to sense wisps of elation from deep within that will inevitably draw your soul to enlightenment.

When you can flow with change, without resisting it, a new world will open before your very eyes. A quiet, nonresistant mind is the means to heightened perceptions, permitting your soul to experience the soft breeze of refined reasoning, allowing a sharper awareness and a more confident composure to come forth.

Inspiration
is born
from a quiet consciousness
and conceived
by divine realization.

Inspiration is born deep within, and is realized by slowing conscious awareness to a calm point at the surface of the mind. When the surface of the mind is bustling with too many thoughts, the subtlety of inspiration is lost in confusion. The faint whispers of true nature are drowned out by the thunder from a mind with little or no control; the capacity to sense who you really are is unclear and uncertain. Attempting to create yourself in conformity with an intellectual template of some kind, a preconceived idea of who you think you should be, falls short—something is always missing. Grasping your true nature with your intellect is like trying to catch the wind in your hand: you can feel it but you cannot hold it.

How do you draw in the wisps of freedom from your true nature, when they seem so nebulous?

By relaxing. Let them become you. Remember, what you are looking for is already within you. With patience, you will witness the evolution of your own consciousness. You will glimpse the silent miracle of inspiration and the pathway to your true spiritual nature.

When consciousness moves from the finite space of brain function to the infinite space of your big mind, you till your spiritual soil in preparation for the seeds of inspiration. When they sprout, enlightenment is born.

*The initial awareness
of your true spiritual nature
is a loving smile
emanating from deep within
your heart and soul.*

When you identify your true nature for the first time, you will sense it as traces of elated energy, growing in time to a broad and lasting smile from deep within. These feelings are captivating, and when you pay attention to them, a wonderful association forms between conscious awareness and the deeper you. The signal your true nature sends is an impulse to smile for no particular reason, usually when you least expect it. Joyfulness will bubble up from within, encouraging laughter. Antiquated ways of manufacturing happiness become obsolete because you no longer need to create what you already feel. The energy from your true nature does not have to be manufactured or maintained; it is the essence of your being. It will slowly dawn on you that what you have been seeking is already within you.

Each time you direct your conscious awareness within and become still, you connect with yourself. With each passing day your insights about who you really are become enhanced, seemingly out of nowhere. This new perception is your pathway to self-understanding and peace of mind, while lighting the way to your enlightenment.

The signature of true nature is effortless effort and an ease in living, filling you with contentment and no need to hurry. What you seek is what you feel: a oneness with yourself and a oneness with all things. When you sense your true spiritual nature, you will smile without a reason and understand why a loving heart makes you smile so often.

*Double happiness
is the ultimate form
of earthly contentment.*

Most people know only the singular form of happiness; that is associated with achieving success in the outside world. But there is a far greater happiness within. Singular happiness is fleeting, requiring perpetual effort and typically based on pleasing or seeking approval from others in circumstances outside your control. Relying on happiness from the outside world has major disadvantages because you may not win another's approval, no matter what you do.

Can you be happy if your need for approval is overlooked by another because of his own internal problems? Depending on happiness from outside you is disappointment waiting to happen.

The QM Practice teaches another way: double happiness—the ultimate form of contentment. Double happiness is a result of consciously connecting with your big mind, deep within your kelee cone. As your true nature emerges, an unmistakable feeling from within begins to appear; it is soul-stirring bliss, craving nothing. Your spiritual essence yearns for nothing physical or material because it is not of this world. In bliss, you will not be distracted by the craving and clinging associated with the material world.

Can you imagine what it is like to feel so good in your soul that nothing in the outside world can compare to how you feel within?

When this occurs, double happiness is realized. When you can embrace your true nature, your soul will give rise to double happiness.

*The infallible truth
of our true spiritual nature
is absolute love and compassion
for all beings.*

No sane person will dispute that love and compassion for your fellowman are spiritual qualities, but how do you recognize a truly spiritual person?

If Jesus had not performed miracles, would you think he was spiritual?

If Buddha had not taught his eightfold path, would you think he was enlightened?

All true spiritual masters teach the same message: Jesus taught us to love one another; Buddha said that the way to attain a compassionate heart is by liberating oneself from selfish craving.

True spirituality is soothing. Watch carefully what comes out of your own mouth; if it is demeaning, unloving, or interfering, it is not spiritual. Attempting to control another's destiny against his wishes is not spiritual. It breaks the prime directive of noninterference. This directive is not an earthly law but an unwritten spiritual mandate and applies to everyone. The penalty for breaking this law is disharmony within the mind. If your disharmony extends into the outside world, civil law must take control because you cannot.

The true spiritual nature of our being does not harm; it heals. The instant you consciously connect with your true nature, a glow begins to replace the gloom within your mind. Your own inner light brightens your day without you doing a single thing except feeling the magnificence of your presence. The path to your true nature is an unmistakable trail because it moves toward inner-harmony. Once found, it will gently lead you to love and compassion for all beings.

*The true spiritual nature of your being
is boundless energy and changeless change;
it is emptiness and fulfillment
at the same time,
unimaginable and yet realizable.*

Everyone in some way is looking for a sense of self-fulfillment. The ways in which we go about getting it are many and varied, some brief in duration while others last for a lifetime.

Short-term gratification is pursued through food, drink, sex, drugs, and material possessions. Indulgence can make us feel good temporarily, but when we try to increase the pleasurable effects and fall into excess, something goes wrong. Any form of enjoyment linked to craving brings about a momentary high and then long-term suffering. The main reason people cross the line of moderation into addiction is because they possess little or no connection to their true spiritual nature. Lacking a connection to one's true nature produces feelings of internal barrenness and loneliness and causes one to constantly seek pleasure to the point of addiction. When you find your true nature, you will never hunger again.

To experience self-regulating, nondepleting well-being, you must access the subtle energy of your true nature. The energy of your spiritual essence cannot be experienced through the physical body, because the energy of true nature is not based on physical laws. Your spiritual essence cannot be understood through intellectualization; it must be experienced through direct contact. The true nature of your being can only be detected by receptive conscious awareness.

The true nature of your being is always there for you, when your sensitivity is attuned to perceive its presence. When your conscious awareness can discern your true nature's presence, you will experience wonder and awe beyond imagination.

The struggle of mankind
is to find
what it already has.

The decision to contemplate the nature of your being is a wise one: It leads to insight. But do not strive too hard to find what is yours by nature. Deep within you is the way to realize your true spiritual essence; you must simply learn to feel it and consciously become it with every fiber of your being. Your true nature is that quintessential space that everyone touches from time to time, where everything is in its place and all is right in the world; yet, for most, the feeling is fleeting, with few individuals knowing how to find this space on command.

Every human being is part of nature, but many do not recognize it. This is why it can be a struggle to feel at home and secure in yourself. When you cannot sense the true nature of your being, you will roam without purpose, hoping, wishing, or praying for a way to find what is closer than you realize.

How long will you search outside yourself for something that can only be found within?

Have you ever sincerely attempted to still your mind?

Start today, by doing The QM Practice for a few minutes, and, upon returning from the still point, gaze upon yourself. Simply observe yourself. Do not try to make thoughts and feelings happen; allow your true nature to bestow what is already there. Touching your true nature is like touching love that endlessly flows. When you finally relinquish the struggle in the outside world and sit still for a few minutes each day, the light of your true nature will slowly dawn on you like a warm sunrise after a long cold night.

*Before enlightenment,
trusting in your heart
is a painful struggle
simply because you cannot
give and receive love without conditions.*

There are many misconceptions about enlightenment. Enlightenment does not mean you understand everything in the outside physical world. Enlightenment means you achieve your own *individual, personal, spiritual perfection*. Enlightenment is the full and complete realization that you are absolute love and free to live in harmony with all nature.

Before enlightenment, there is an awareness in your soul that something is missing—you cannot put your finger on it, but you can feel an incompleteness. Your incompleteness is telling you that your spiritual puzzle has missing pieces. Someone whose spiritual puzzle is nearing completion consistently exhibits kindness and loving behavior, whereas a less-developed soul with a large number of missing spiritual pieces tends to have difficulty maintaining harmony.

Upon finding all of the missing pieces of your personal spiritual puzzle, a great burden will be lifted from your soul and the ability to give and receive love without holding back will be yours. To attain an enlightened state of mind, you must realize why you are unable to give or receive love, even though you hunger for it.

But how do you love? Consciously stop fighting your capacity to feel harmony!

The giving and receiving of love is multifaceted; it is the greatest of all lessons to learn and also the most painful. You must open your heart completely. You must expose your heart, risk being hurt, and accept love into your soul. You must learn to trust your heart. Once love is realized in your heart, you will understand that love can never abandon you; it cannot, because it is who you really are.

At the moment of full enlightenment,
you will realize
that this is it!
This is it!

At the moment of full enlightenment comes the realization that your dues are paid and you are free to love without constraints. Enlightenment is not some lofty spiritual concept, it is the attainment of absolute love! You will never have to be anything other than who you are, because you are love. Your heart is your home and is experienced with every fiber of your loving being. You fully comprehend every facet of love and feel compassion for everyone and everything. The ability to love completely has always been in you, but up until this point you did not know how to open your soul to its majesty!

When the blessed event finally occurs and you are released from the bonds of ignorance, you have the opportunity to experience love like you never have before. The feeling of love and freedom is off any scale measured by the human brain. At this point, a striking thought will overwhelm you. *This is it! This is it! The experience of life is now!* You will realize that every single moment of life is yours to experience.

The price of attaining enlightenment is in pain and suffering, from which love and compassion are eventually born. It would be wonderful if it was not so, but all you can do is continue to live and learn until you reach the ultimate spiritual goal.

After enlightenment,
you realize that your heart is your home;
you have freed yourself
from the confinements of ignorance
by becoming absolute love.

After enlightenment, when the debt of suffering is paid in full, you will realize that absolute love is complete freedom. There is no need to hurry from place to place, as each moment offers its own new realization.

All that remains after enlightenment is the accumulation of intellectual knowledge, while at the same time enjoying every moment of your life. The ego-driven belief that knowledge would somehow make you superior is no longer a consideration. Nothing in the world outside can compare with what you experience within. At this point knowledge is simply used as a tool to help your fellow beings on their pathway.

Enlightenment is a silent victory which cannot truly be expressed with words. But it can be shared through the vibration of one who has experienced it. The realization of full enlightenment transforms your soul into a moving expression of compassion, beauty, and love. You walk your pathway with patience, quietly teaching what you know to those who will listen.

Everyone is on a path toward enlightenment, whether they realize it or not. Those who realize it simply suffer less and love more. The choice to free yourself is yours and no one else's.

The Three P's of The QM Practice:
1. Practice: Do your meditation.
2. Persistence: Practice diligently,
even when you do not feel like it.
3. Patience: Frustration indicates
more practice and patience
are needed.

The Quiescence Meditation Practice

*Find a place in your home
that can become a sanctuary
from the cares and worries
of the outside world.*

The Quiescence Meditation Practice

Find a place to do your practice that is peaceful and conducive to tranquillity.

A quiet place is a sanctuary for your soul. Find a comfortable place to do your meditation, but do not restrict doing your practice only to your favorite place. If you feel secure meditating only in your sanctuary, it becomes a ritual and will limit your ability to practice anywhere. A routine is good as long as it is not absolute. The biggest distraction while meditating will be noise. When you can detach from sense consciousness in a noisy place, your mind gains strength and becomes more focused. As you progress in letting go of your senses, you will be able to do your practice almost anywhere.

Free your mind from the outside world.

Before you do your practice, turn off all outside distractions such as radios, television sets, phones, and pagers. Use your answering machine to help organize your time, do not become a slave to your telephone.

Inform anyone who may interrupt you that this is your quiet time and to please not disturb you. When those around you begin to see the benefits from your calmness, they will learn to honor your need for sanctuary.

*Meditate in the silence of the morning
before the activity of your mind begins,
and in the quiet of the evening
before becoming too tired.*

Meditate early in the morning when the outside world is quiet.

Practice meditating before your mind becomes active and invents excuses for why other things need doing. The intellect can think of countless reasons why you do not have time to meditate; this is the time when you need to meditate the most! Once patterns in your brain start moving, they do not like to stop. Behavior patterns feed off adrenaline-based energy and do not want to relinquish control to your conscious awareness.

Do you ever notice when you are thinking, that it is as if there are two of you? One part is your brain—or small mind—which likes to think and do, and the other part is your big mind, which likes to experience and feel. Your big mind is the detached, nonlinear part of your spiritual essence whose sense of accomplishment comes from simple enjoyment and inner contentment rather than productivity at any cost.

Meditate in the evening before you get too tired.

If you are a person who is exhausted at the end of the day, do your practice earlier in the evening before you get too weary. It is a bad habit to meditate and fall asleep. You are training your mind to become still, not to sleep. In the early stages of learning to meditate, it is very important to make a clear distinction between sleep and stillness. If you are not sure if you fell asleep or if you were meditating, examine how you feel when you come back to full awareness; if you are groggy, you were drifting into sleep. If you are alert and wide-awake upon return, you were meditating properly.

Sitting in meditation
with your spine erect
is not the mark of an enlightened man
but of one who is diligent and aspiring
to reach enlightenment.

Proper posture is good discipline.

Sitting with your spine erect is correct posture, a good habit and the way to teach your mind the difference between meditation and nodding off or wandering without control. When your spine is erect, it signals your mind to remain in a relaxed state but not to sleep. If you lie down to meditate, your brain will probably signal your awareness to become drowsy, because this is the position you assume when you sleep. You already know how to sleep; you are learning to meditate. Sleep is permitting your awareness to spread out into unconsciousness, while Quiescence Meditation is allowing your conscious awareness to be in a state of one-pointed stillness without drifting.

Sitting in a comfortable position is the absence
of distraction.

It is not necessary to sit in a cross-legged or lotus position to practice Quiescence Meditation. It is perfectly acceptable to sit in a chair with your feet flat on the floor.

Balance your head in an effortless-effort position.

How you hold your head during meditation is very important. It can be a major distraction if it falls forward or backward, straining your neck muscles. Tilt your head forward and back a few times until you feel the position where your head is balanced naturally; this is the "effortless-effort" position. Once again, this is simply basic good posture.

*The breath
is to the physical
what silence
is to the spiritual:
essential.*

Breathing is a natural function of being.

There are many meditation practices that concentrate on the breath as a focal point of awareness. Breathing is essential for the physical body, but to access deeper states of mind, the breath must be allowed to be at a resting state, much as it is while sleeping. In The QM Practice you simply breathe normally. As you detach from sense consciousness, your breathing will naturally decrease to a resting state. In this state of being your body's aging process slows, which ultimately lengthens your life.

What to do with your hands?

It seems many people do not know what to do with their hands. It is not necessary to have a special position for your hands other than being relaxed and comfortable. I prefer to have my hands resting in my lap palms up, simply because it feels natural. Once again, the goal is to be free of sense-consciousness distractions.

*Being physically comfortable is necessary to do
The Practice correctly.*

Wear clothing that will not distract you. If your clothing is too tight, your brain will register tension, which will divert your attention and make it difficult to calm down. If you cannot let go of sense consciousness, physical tension will not allow you to drop into the deeper states of mind.

The eyes may be the window to the soul,
but one does not have to be looking
through the window all of the time.

Relax and allow your eyes to rest during your practice.

It is a common problem with students to have difficulty closing their eyes during their practice; tension from thought prevents the eyes from relaxing. After all, your eyes are at the surface of your mind, the central location where thoughts are generated. Typically, eyestrain is caused because people work too long and fill their lives with more activities than they need to. Anytime you cross the line of moderation, something in your life will suffer.

When students begin to meditate, they may be startled to realize how much stress their eyes are carrying. When people exert excessive amounts of adrenaline-based analytical energy at the surface of the mind, the eyes will be overworked.

Eyestrain during meditation can be a major distraction. Relaxing your brain network and calming the surface of your mind relieves considerable pressure from the eyes and is physically and mentally therapeutic.

If you are unable to softly and gently close your eyes, you are not relaxed and light coming from the outside world will tend to draw your awareness to the surface of your mind and the thinking process. Eyestrain is a physical form of tension which will not allow your conscious awareness to drop into your kelee cone, where detachment and true respite for the mind are found. With much practice over a period of time, all tension problems associated with the eyes can be overcome.

*Calming the brain
relaxes the physical body.*

When brain function calms, the physical body relaxes.

When thought activity in your brain races, it does not allow you to calm your conscious awareness and it is impossible to relax your physical body. It is of great benefit to detach from sense consciousness to ease tension in the physical body. The world of sense consciousness is filled with stress, i.e., glare to the eyes, loud noises to the ears, anything that is offensive to the physical senses. The muscle structure of the body works off of tension, but if the muscular system is not allowed to rest, it grows fatigued. Finding the point of moderation is vital. The key is quieting the mind and not inflicting undue pressure on the body. In this practice, you ultimately want to be aware of nothing—complete stillness of mind without the distractions of the outward senses.

Conscious awareness changes as it moves from an intellectual function at the surface of the mind into the timeless realm below the surface. All on the planet who are seeking spiritual fulfillment are looking for this realm or state of mind, and it is within everyone. It is found by exploring your kelee cone and your relationship to your spiritual essence. It starts with quiescence, a quiet state, and evolves into a quintessential state, which is the purest state anyone can be—absolute love.

*Conscious awareness
is knowing
what you are doing
while you are doing it.*

Locating your conscious awareness on command.

When thought activity is calm, you can learn to feel your conscious awareness on command. If I ask you to *feel your fingertips*, your conscious awareness will automatically go there. If I say *bring your conscious awareness to the top of your head*, your awareness will go there. Where you direct your attention is where your conscious awareness will be.

Step One: For about two minutes, bring your conscious awareness to the top of your head and allow it to descend, by feeling it as a horizontal plane of awareness relaxing through both hemispheres of the brain down to the surface of the mind.

The left and right hemispheres of the brain are where the chatter of the mind is generated; this chatter is what needs to be calmed. Step One of The Practice is especially therapeutic for dissipating mental tension and stress.

Without training, most people are subject to pattern-driven programs and do not have an independent, free-conscious awareness, so ignorance unknowingly creates problems. Because of the complexity of the brain, conscious awareness can be a mass of images, with racing thoughts and very little actual accomplishment. Ignorance is transformed into mindfulness when one becomes an independent conscious observer, aware of one's actions rather than being ruled by negative patterns from the past.

*The QM Practice
opens your mind
to one of the greatest gifts
you can give yourself:
experiencing the silent miracles of life.*

The QM Practice becomes self-explanatory through the enlightenment of your own mind.

As the chatter in your brain diminishes, your sensitivity to subtle energy increases. As your conscious awareness sharpens and becomes more focused, you become aware of the electrochemical energy of your mind. You begin to sense the difference between hard analytical energy and the soft subtle energy which allows your conscious awareness to feel your mind with greater clarity.

Step Two: When your conscious awareness is relaxed at the surface of your mind, you can descend into the kelee cone of energy that is the entrance to your soul. Remain at a still point in your kelee cone for about three minutes and then come back to the surface of your mind to full awareness.

As you drop within, mind function detaches from brain function and an independent observer emerges. This independent observer is composed of subtle energy and becomes the light of awareness which illumines the darkness of negative emotion trapped in your soul. When conscious awareness no longer has to put up walls to protect itself from fear-based dysfunction, you do not mentally feed it and the dysfunction must then consume itself, completely dissolving. As this negative energy dissipates, your overall vibration is transformed, changing your whole being. As you become aware of who you are without fear, a miracle begins to happen: you feel the true spiritual essence of your being appear from within.

*The surface of the mind
is where
brain function meets mind function.*

The surface of the mind is the primary reference point in The QM Practice.

If you pay attention to *where* you are understanding what you are reading right now, you will notice that you can feel where your thinking is located; it is a horizontal plane of electrochemical energy exactly at eye level. This is the proverbial and literal surface of your mind. This plane of energy is where brain function and mind function meet. The area on top of the surface has to do with thinking and the area below the surface has to do with feeling. If I say *think or feel the surface of your mind*, your awareness automatically goes there. Being aware of this reference point, and the ability to calm it, will open the entrance to your heart and soul.

Setting your mind's biological clock.

Setting your biological clock is as simple as instructing yourself to return to full awareness at a specific time; your mind will automatically call you back. This inherent timing mechanism is what many people use to wake up at a certain time each morning or what signals them to go to bed each evening. Your biological clock is a useful tool when you are in deeper states of meditation, below the surface of your mind, where linear time does not exist. In the kelee cone there is no sensation of time, so the biological clock is needed to bring you back, which in this practice occurs after approximately three minutes.

Note: Once you have been doing The Practice for a while, setting your biological clock is an instruction you do not have to think about; it becomes an automatic response.

*Dropping your conscious awareness
into the entrance
of your soul.*

The heart of The QM Practice is found below the surface of the mind in the kelee cone.

Within all of us is a field of electrochemical energy that is the entrance to the soul. It is where your conscious awareness is free from the constraints of the brain network or the conditioning from your past. In this cone of energy you will find the key to unlock the chains that bind you in habitual patterns. In this field of energy, below the surface of the mind, all heartaches and happiness reside.

The foremost component of The QM Practice is in learning to calm your conscious awareness and allowing it to relax down below the surface of your mind until you come to a natural stopping point in your kelee cone. When you reach this stopping point, keep all of your awareness together and remain quiet for about three minutes. You will stop naturally, at a resting point, or where resistance is within you. Resistance can range from anything you dislike about yourself to an incident that was mistakenly taken to heart.

One of the first observations you will make when doing this part of the practice is, *If I am down here, who is up there?* and the minute you have this thought your conscious awareness will return to the surface of your mind. With practice you will learn to be still in your kelee cone, free from the distractions of the outside world.

Note: Do not look around with your mind's eye when in your kelee cone, because part of your conscious awareness will start to think and you will return to the surface of your mind. Once again, Step Two of The Practice is to remain at a still point in your kelee cone for about three minutes and then come back to the surface of your mind, to full awareness.

*Upon returning to full awareness
from meditation,
review your practice through introspection,
then take time for contemplation.*

The Three Principles of The QM Practice.

1. Meditation

Do The Practice. The hardest thing about The Practice is to simply do it. The QM Practice takes approximately ten minutes twice a day, which is only one percent of your day. Never will you put so little into something and receive so much in return. The Practice is a maintenance program for cleansing the mind and at the same time awakening the soul.

2. Introspection

Step Three: Upon returning from meditation, review what you remember from your practice for about five minutes.

The introspection portion of The Practice is for retrospective observational purposes, to evaluate your meditation. The time you devote to introspection will teach you a great deal about who you are. If you are visualizing, observing, or planning while meditating, you are thinking and not doing The Practice. It is difficult to completely still your mind on command! The discipline of reaching stillness is an ongoing process. Do not let your frustrations weigh you down. Be kind, but absolutely truthful when you grade the quality of your meditation.

3. Contemplation

This is the time to review how you are changing as your dis-harmony is released. Questions to ask are: *How do I feel about my practice* and *What changes am I noticing in my waking state?* I recommend students write in their journal. I advise them to ponder how they feel and to record their thoughts. As time passes, you will be amazed at how you have grown and changed.

The Quiescence Meditation Practice

Step One: Approximately two minutes.

Sit down, get comfortable, and begin relaxing your brain activity. Bring your conscious awareness to the top of your head and *feel* it as a horizontal plane of awareness relaxing down through both hemispheres of your brain to the surface of your mind. Be consciously relaxed, but not thinking.

Step Two: Approximately three minutes.

Relax and allow your awareness to drop below the surface of your mind into your kelee cone to a still point within. The goal is to let go of sense consciousness and experience total stillness before returning to full consciousness.

   Note: Before you drop from the surface of your mind, set your biological clock to bring you back to complete awareness in about three minutes.

Step Three: Approximately five minutes.

Upon returning to the surface of your mind, reflect on what you noticed about your practice. Do not bolt into your day.

Pace yourself. Do your practice for ten minutes in the morning and evening to the best of your ability and get into the experience of your life. Allow the true nature of your being to unfold.

Recommendation

Keep a journal to write your experiences and record your progress. You think you will remember everything, but I can assure you, you will forget many subtle gems of wisdom about how you have grown.

The Ins and Outs of
The Quiescence Meditation Practice

1. Be kind to yourself. Give yourself the gift of a clear mind—meditate.

2. Do your practice for ten minutes in the morning and ten minutes in the evening. Allow the effects from The Practice to manifest themselves throughout the day.

3. The QM Practice takes twenty minutes out of twenty-four hours, which is only one percent of your day. If you do not have one percent of twenty-four hours to cleanse the instrument running your whole life, how much self-control do you have?

4. If you are slow to wake up in the morning or too tired at bedtime, do your practice whenever possible, until you become accustomed to a morning and evening routine.

5. In Step One of The Practice, relax your conscious awareness from the top of your head down to the surface of the mind without consciously thinking for about two minutes. *Feel* a distinction between a softened conscious awareness and the tension in the brain network. The goal is to have a relaxed conscious awareness without thoughts.

6. When your conscious awareness reaches the surface of the mind, do not worry if you do not drop below the surface into your kelee cone; you are only experiencing your own resistance. When your resistance breaks down, you will drop. Be patient.

7. Set your biological clock for about three minutes before you drop into your kelee cone. This becomes automatic after the first few times.

8. The time you are in your kelee cone is not the time to investigate what you see and experience! If you are thinking or spacing out, your conscious awareness cannot not be still. *Stillness is the objective of The Practice.*

9. If you are falling asleep while meditating, you are either too tired or too relaxed. When your conscious awareness is too relaxed, it will spread out and wander. Refocus by pulling all of your awareness to a pinpoint within you. The sleep/stillness distinction takes time to master. Do The Practice to the best of your ability.

10. Once you return to the surface of your mind, you can look back at what you remember about your practice. Keep a journal to record your experiences.

11. Do your practice even when you do not feel like it; this is when you need to do it the most.

12. The rewards received from The Practice are experienced as mindfulness in your daily activities. Once again, total stillness in your practice is the goal, with enlightenment ultimately becoming your conscious way of being.

13. If you have not given The Practice at least six months, you have not really given it a chance.

14. It is not unusual to feel a small drop in physical energy after beginning The Practice, as you wean your mind off hard analytical adrenaline-based energy. This feeling is transitory. After a short period of time your energy level will stabilize into an overall feeling of calmness, and you will have a new understanding of subtle energy.

15. When you begin to drop your walls, you may feel some emotional discomfort—this is known as "processing." Processing is what most people call a mood. When the discomfort or mood passes, you will not experience that particular dysfunction again.

16. When you are processing, be kind to yourself. You may want to sleep more than usual. This is normal. Give yourself a mental-health day, if you can. If not, pace yourself throughout your day.

17. From time to time you will experience physiological effects when processing, such as headaches, heartaches, nausea, low energy, or anxiety. If a button was linked with physical dis-

comfort at the time it was formed, it will mimic the same response when it is being processed out. Any physical discomfort
will cease when the dysfunction is released. Everyone occasionally experiences physiological discomfort. Compartmentalized
electrochemical dysfunction is at the nucleus of psychosomatic
illness.

18. *Sumadhi* occurs when the space occupied by dysfunction is replaced by the true nature of your being. *Sumadhi* is a
reward for your diligence, a potent, natural, euphoric feeling,
stimulating an awareness of oneness with all things.

19. Mindfulness develops as your conscious awareness
rises to a new level.

20. This practice will slow down the aging process. Each
time you still your mind, degeneration declines, thereby allowing the physical body to rejuvenate. It is known that people
who meditate are the longest-living people on the planet.

21. Efficiency will increase because your conscious awareness is not scattered, thereby naturally improving your ability
to focus without distraction.

22. Depression will decrease. Worry, sadness, and degradation of oneself will plummet.

23. As negative, energy-draining programs are deleted, the
immune system is free to function at optimum power.

24. A deeper self-awareness enhances relationships at home and work with the ability to give from the heart without expecting anything in return.

25. Once you find the entrance to your soul and your kelee cone, you will find your heart and never be lost again. As long as you continue to go within and be still each day, you will always be on your spiritual path.

26. The Three Disciplines of The QM Practice are: Meditation, Introspection, and Contemplation.

27. The Three P's of Quiescence Meditation are: Practice, Persistence, and Patience.

About the Author

The author began his formal studies in 1978 at a spiritual church in Encinitas, California. It was there that he met a teacher who taught meditation—stillness of the mind. His studies included all Eastern and Western philosophies and the golden thread of truth that runs throughout all cultures. In February 1990 he was ordained a minister of The Chapel of Awareness Spiritual Church. In March 1992 he went on sabbatical to study in seclusion and write *The Way Is Within*.

The Quiescence Meditation Practice was born in 1985 from Ron's personal spiritual development and began to take shape during his early years of teaching. He mastered a form of meditation, ascertained from what works and what does not, as a means to help individuals release themselves from the self-defeating mental patterns that block their ability to experience their true spiritual essence. Ron's goal is to give people an easy-to-learn, logical way to understand themselves from the inside out, helping them become aware of a series of electrochemical reference points within the mind. The QM Practice is a proven, practical pathway to enlightenment, open to anyone, regardless of belief systems, religious background, or age, who sincerely wants to end his own suffering and find genuine happiness.

Ron Rathbun and his wife, Lavana, are founders of The Quiescence Meditation Center in Carlsbad, California, where Ron continues to teach and lecture.